Women of Hope

WOMEN OF HOPE

DOCTORS OF THE CHURCH

TERRY POLAKOVIC

Our Sunday Visitor
Huntington, Indiana

Nihil Obstat
Msgr. Michael Heintz, Ph.D.
Censor Librorum

Imprimatur
✠ Kevin C. Rhoades
Bishop of Fort Wayne-South Bend
January 14, 2021

Our Sunday Visitor Publishing Division
Our Sunday Visitor, Inc.
200 Noll Plaza
Huntington, IN 46750
www.osv.com
1-800-348-2440

ISBN: 978-1-68192-434-2 (Inventory No. T2322)
1. RELIGION—Christianity—Saints & Sainthood.
2. RELIGION—Christian Theology—History.
3. RELIGION—Christianity—Catholic.
eISBN: 978-1-68192-435-9
LCCN: 2021930101

Cover design: Tyler Ottinger
Cover art: The Crosiers, Shutterstock
Interior design: Amanda Falk
Interior art: Caroline Baker Mazure

PRINTED IN THE UNITED STATES OF AMERICA

To my husband, Mike, for all his love and support,
and for my grandchildren: Nate, Sophia,
Olivia, and Klara, all future saints and
maybe even Doctors of the Church

Contents

PART FOUR
SAINT HILDEGARD OF BINGEN

Women impregnated with the spirit of the Gospel
can do so much to aid mankind in not falling.

Pope Saint Paul VI, 1965

Introduction

I have often thought that hope is strengthened by remembering. In other words, when things seem desperate, it is good to remember how God has answered our prayers in the past. I was thinking of this during the summer of 2018, when I was in dire need of hope. I needed the kind of hope Pope Francis speaks of in his book *On Hope*, where he tells us, "Hope is not being afraid to see the reality for what it is and accept the contradictions."[1]

At that time, the Catholic faithful, including me, were reeling from yet another report concerning sexual abuse by a priest. But this wasn't just any priest. It was the now-laicized Cardinal Theodore E. McCarrick, the former archbishop of Washington, D.C., and a prominent Roman Catholic voice in international and public policy.

And if that wasn't enough, just two months after the fall of McCarrick, the scathing Pennsylvania Grand Jury Report was released, implicating more than three hundred sex-abuser priests from six different dioceses, all of which had covered up these crimes for decades. Sadly, before the dust settled on these two events, it became clear that sexual abuse cases weren't just covered up in the United States; they were covered up all over the world. In the wake of so many clerical sex abuse scandals, the Catholic Church once again appeared hypocritical and bankrupt, both morally and spiritually.

In the two years that have followed my initial draft of this book, many other scandals have presented themselves. These include more sexual sins, financial mismanagement, the contention surrounding the Synod on the Amazon in 2019, the false imprisonment of a cardinal, and general confusion about all sorts of things. Today, the line between Church and state is razor thin. Perhaps, however, an additional significant blow to faithful Catholics was the closure of the churches in 2020 due to the COVID-19 virus, which made the sacraments — especially the Eucharist, the source and summit of our faith — largely unavailable for most Catholics for many months. No doubt about it, these have been tough years. You would certainly be forgiven if you were disillusioned with the Church.

In trying to make sense of the revelations of 2018, I felt the pangs of despair. This was especially unnerving because by the nature of being a Catholic, I believe in Christian hope, the kind of hope that tells us that no matter what, God is always with us. That is when a friend invited me to turn to the saints, and to remember those holy men and women who are there to help us during times like this. Instead of destroying the Church through scandal, the saints in every age have strengthened the Church. In fact, they have enriched the entire Christian Tradition. The saints offer all of us a model for leaving behind bitterness and negativity and striving instead to remember that the Church — and the world — belongs to God. In other words, the saints are our models of hope, even in the darkest times in our world and within the Church itself.

Taking my friend's advice, I followed through with a dream of mine to learn more about the four women Doctors of the Church: Saint Teresa of Ávila, Saint Catherine of Siena, Saint Thérèse of Lisieux, and Saint Hildegard of Bingen. For some time, I have longed to know them better. In the course of this project, I have dubbed them the "Women of Hope," as the title of this book indicates. Each of these holy women lived in times of tribulation for the Church — times rather like our own, and in many respects, worse. Between them, they survived the Spanish Inquisition, the Black Plague, the Avignon Papacy, Jansenism, and the Albigensian Crusade, and at different points, an utterly corrupt clergy. Despite this, they all persevered through years of sickness, adversity, and ridicule, both from inside and outside of the Church. They fought the good fight right up until the end, and all died as faithful daughters of the Church. Most importantly, they never lost hope.

Having worked for fifteen years in a Catholic women's apostolate that focused on teaching the Faith, I was impressed that each of these four saints had been given the very special title of "Doctor." In this instance, the word *doctor* means *teacher*. Being accorded the title of Doctor of the Church indicates that the writings and teachings of these saints are useful to Christians in any age of the Church. The men and women who have been given this title are also particularly known for their depth of understanding and the orthodoxy of their theological teachings. This does not mean they are infallible, but it does mean that they have contributed significantly to the formulation of Christian teaching in at least one area.

While each of these four women has contributed greatly to the intellectual tradition of our faith, in reality they are primarily teachers of the heart. As I searched for hope in the face of the darkness in the Church today, I at first believed that my resentment would subside and my hope would return if only I could *learn* more. In other words, I believed that head knowledge alone would soften my soul. Unexpectedly, what I learned from Teresa, Catherine, Thérèse, and Hildegard is not head knowledge at all. Instead, they touched my heart with the simple truth that God never abandons his people, but he meets us at the point of our greatest darkness. Time and again, he met each one of them in their darkest hour. He was their hope, and as we know, hope never disappoints (see Rom 5:5). Learning about these four women restored my hope for the Church, and even increased it. Since I began studying, and more importantly praying with, these saints, my life has been richly blessed.

From Teresa, I learned to pray and to wait upon the Lord. She was forty years old when she experienced her true conversion, and from then on, she placed all of her hope and trust in the Lord, where it was very well received. Without Christ using her as his hands and feet, what Teresa accomplished in her life would have simply been impossible.

I also love the passion and wisdom of Catherine. Her zeal for souls is unrivaled. If fact, the combination of her deep love of God and love of neighbor produced hope wherever she went, especially in situations where all seemed lost. She was a true "contemplative in action."

I must admit that Thérèse holds a special place in my heart because I have never read anyone who had a more developed interior life at such a young age. We share a common experience in that we both lost a parent when we were four years old. You never get over an experience like that, but I drew hope and inspiration from her autobiography, *The Story of a Soul*.

Hildegard challenged me in every way possible, and for good reason, as she was the most powerful woman of her era. She could literally do *everything*. In our day and age, it is difficult to grasp the scope of her accomplishments. God used this truly formidable woman to rekindle hope during her life on earth, and she continues to offer us hope in our own day.

Each of these women took the initiative, based on her relationship with God, to launch herself into the life of the Church. Every step they took was a seed of hope. They each heard a call from God, and they answered it, trusting that the love of God, which was the center of their lives, would carry them through any difficulty. They had hope in God's goodness and his providential care for his Church in their time, and their message remains timely, their stories worth telling.

There is one final point that I would like to mention, and it is about the ordering of the chapters in this book. Rather than write about these women in chronological order, I ordered the chapters based upon the date when each woman received the title "Doctor of the Church." I did this for two reasons. First of all, everything in the Church makes much more sense when it is taken in context. By this I mean that there were certain events taking place in the world that made the timing perfect. Think of Pope Paul VI naming Teresa and Catherine as Doctors in 1970, right after the formation of the women's liberation movement and the sexual revolution of the 1960s. Secondly, we can only hope that one day in the future, there will be other women joining these four, so this ordering will allow this story to continue!

Part One
Saint Teresa
of Ávila

*Hope, O my soul, hope. You know neither the day
nor the hour. Watch carefully, for everything passes
quickly, even though your impatience makes doubtful
what is certain, and turns a very short time into
a long one. Dream that the more you struggle, the
more you prove the love that you bear God, and the
more you will rejoice one day with your Beloved,
in a happiness and rapture that can never end.*

WOMAN OF PRAYER

There are few things more delightful in this life than a soul who is deeply, wildly in love with God, a soul who can confidently say, "Thy will be done," and mean it. In Teresa of Jesus, known to us as Saint Teresa of Ávila, we find such a soul. Nicknamed "Big Teresa" because of her towering personality and tremendous contribution to the Church (and to distinguish her from Thérèse, the Little Flower), Teresa had a voracious appetite for life, and a subtle and endearing wit, in which she exhibited the twin qualities of humility and humor. Perhaps better than most, she recognized that humor makes life bearable. It "allows us to break but not shatter."[1] This attitude allowed her to forge many a new frontier out of her sheer love of Christ and his kingdom here on earth.

A strikingly beautiful woman, with the passion that marked her Spanish heritage, Teresa found her place not only among the great Spanish saints, but also with the flamenco dancers and bullfighters whose rough, uncomplicated energy exceeds the most extraordinary human limitations. Some say to understand and appreciate Saint Teresa, we must look at Castile, the land of her birth. "Its wind-swept plains, its granite boulders, its bitter winters, and sun-scorched summers were the womb that nourished [a young Teresa]. A gentler landscape might not have produced a woman of such courage and determination. ... [Castile] speaks of hardship and danger, of struggle and tenacity, of time and eternity, of life and death."[2]

Teresa's natural gifts were enhanced by God's grace and glory, and as a result, Teresa of Jesus has become the ideal spiritual mentor for the whole world — a woman whose reputation for holiness and wisdom has no boundaries of any kind. She is loved by Catholics and non-Catholics alike. She was canonized in 1662 by Pope Gregory XV, and was declared the first woman

Doctor of the Church by Pope Paul VI in 1970. Today we revere her as the Doctor of Prayer. In his encyclical letter *Spe Salvi* (On Christian Hope), Pope Benedict XVI wrote: "The first essential setting for learning hope is prayer."[3] Indeed, Teresa teaches us to pray and thereby to hope. Throughout her life, the infused theological virtue of hope compelled her onward to trust in Christ's promises and his unfailing help. Through her own widening horizons, Teresa has made it possible for each of us to hope in ways that we may never have dreamed of on our own.

FAMILY LIFE

Like all of us, Saint Teresa's journey began at a given time and place. It was her father, Don Alonso Sanchez de Cepeda, who first recorded the details of her birth. Using a small notebook, one brief but unforgettable entry reads: "On Wednesday, the twenty-eighth of March 1515, at five o'clock in the morning within a half hour or so of daybreak, my daughter Teresa was born."[4] Little did he realize that because of her, his name would go down in the annals of history as the father of one of the greatest saints of all time. Named Teresa de Cepeda y Ahumada, after her maternal grandmother, she was the third child born to Doña Beatriz de Ahumada and Don Alonso Sanchez de Cepeda. Alonso was a widower with two children when he married fourteen-year-old Beatriz in 1509. Together they had ten children, resulting in a bustling, devout Catholic family of fourteen.

Despite the fact that she was one of twelve children, Teresa enjoyed an exceptionally close relationship with her mother. In her autobiography, *The Book of Her Life*, Teresa offers us a glimpse of her mother: "Although very beautiful, she never gave occasion to anyone to think she paid any attention to her beauty. ... Her clothes were those of a much older person. She was very gentle and very intelligent. Great were the trials she suffered during her life."[5] Beatriz had but one vice, which she shared with her children but hid from her husband. Much to his dismay, she loved to read books about chivalry and romance, which he believed was an inappropriate pastime for a woman of her station. Teresa and her brothers enjoyed the excitement of these stories just as much as their mother.

In addition to reading romance novels, Teresa and her brother Rodrigo (a few years older) loved reading the lives of saints. In fact, from a very early age, they both fantasized about going straight to heaven through the triumph of martyrdom. Teresa wrote about this in her autobiography, telling us that when she was about seven years old, she persuaded Rodrigo to go with her to the land of the Moors "and beg them, out of love of God, to cut off [their heads]."[6] They set out from Ávila to gain this swift attainment of heaven, but their plans were foiled when an uncle found them and brought them home.

As with most Castilian families during that era, life revolved around the father, the man of the house. Indeed, Teresa's father, Alonso, was the pivotal figure in the lives of his wife, children, and the many servants within his household. He was a formidable person with a devout and commanding personality. Teresa adored her father, and whenever she spoke of him, she praised him for his charity to the poor, his compassion toward the sick, his honesty, and most especially, for the attention he showered on her. In fact, she was not the least bit shy in claiming that "I was the most loved by my father."[7]

At the time of Teresa's birth, the Cepeda family was living a life of luxury and privilege. Their stately home was located just inside the city walls, and it was a splendid, rambling mansion with patios and gardens, horses, and even sheep. Within this mansion, Beatriz and Alonso created a loving and devout family atmosphere. They intentionally structured their home around Christian practices, beginning with morning prayer and daily Mass. The whole family prayed the Angelus three times a day, and they said grace before meals. While they were eating, they took turns reading passages aloud from the lives of the saints.

Sadly, this chapter of Teresa's life ended with the death of her beloved mother. Beatriz was only thirty-three years old when she finally succumbed to a lengthy illness, leaving a young and devastated Teresa. This was just the first of many times when Teresa's life would be forever changed. In her autobiography, she tells us that in her grief, she sought the protection of the Blessed Mother:

> I remember that when my mother died, I was twelve years old or a little less. When I began to understand what I had lost, I went, afflicted, before an image of our Lady and besought her with so many tears to be my mother. It seems to me that although I did this with simplicity, it helped me. For I have found favor with the sovereign Virgin in everything I have asked of her, and in the end, she has drawn me to herself.[8]

The death of her mother influenced Teresa not only during this lonely time, but every day for the rest of her life. In a very real way, childhood as she understood it was over. The time had come for her to begin the pilgrimage into young adulthood. And, like many of us, her journey was a challenging one, in which she made her share of mistakes.

A Difficult Adolescence

A mother's death is a devastating loss for a family, especially for children who are still in need of maternal care. In Teresa's case, although she was old enough to care for herself, she was at that critical juncture between childhood and womanhood, when a young girl needs her mother the most. It is not surprising that without this important supervision and gentle correction, Teresa looked to others for encouragement and support. She found a mentor and model in a wayward cousin who was older and well-acquainted with the ways of the world. A better choice for this kind of companion would surely have been Teresa's older sister, Maria (likely the person her mother would have picked). Unfortunately, Maria's upcoming wedding and her preoccupation with planning the affair prevented her from filling this important role for young Teresa.

On her own, Teresa set out on the rocky path of worldly desire and vain pursuits. Determined to look pretty and to follow her cousin's lead, she began to dress extravagantly, indulging herself with perfumes and potions, and spending countless hours caring for her hands and hair. To be sure, she was proud of her natural beauty and her ability to attract attention from others. Her striking features are described in the following passage in the introduction[9] to her autobiography:

> She was medium in height and tended to be more plump than thin. Her unusual face could not be described as either round or aquiline; the skin was white and the cheeks flesh-colored. Her forehead was broad, her eyebrows somewhat thick, their dark brown color having a reddish tinge. Her eyes were black, lively, and round, not very large but well placed and protruding a little.
>
> The nose was small; the mouth medium in size and delicately shaped, and her chin was well proportioned. The white teeth sparkled and were equal in size. Three tiny moles, considered highly ornamental in those days, added further grace to her appearance; one below

the center of the nose, the second over the left side of the mouth, the third beneath the mouth on the same side. Her hair was shining black and gently curled.[10]

Without the grounding of her mother's wise counsel, Teresa became centered on herself, both physically and emotionally. The seeds of vanity and physical attraction had been sown early due to her exposure to romance novels and tales of chivalry. Now that she was older, she longed to be loved and adored like the beautiful and tragic women in those familiar stories, and as a result, she fell into foolish conversations and flirtations. Before long, her behavior began to jeopardize her reputation, as well as her father's and her elder brother's standing in the community.

At the time this was happening, Alonso was a forty-eight-year-old widower with eleven children still living at home. Initially, he turned a blind eye to his favorite daughter's shortcomings, refusing to address this dire state of affairs. Teresa recognized this, and later in her life she would write about this situation:

> So excessive was the love my father bore me and so great my [disguise] that he was unable to believe that there was something wrong with me, and so he was not angered with me. Since this period of time had been brief, and though he knew something, nothing could be said with certainty. For since I feared so much for my honor, I used every effort to keep my actions secret, and I never considered that one can never do this with Him who sees all things.[11]

Even though he would have preferred to overlook Teresa's behavior, Alonso finally admitted that she was in need of help. He decided it was time to make a change, and when she reached the age of sixteen, he sent her to the Augustinian Convent of Our Lady of Grace to further her education. The nuns who operated this boarding school accepted girls of nobility to help prepare them for marriage. Here, the students "were not expected to acquire much academic education beyond reading and writing; rather they were encouraged to be virtuous, to become familiar with the Catechism, to keep accounts, embroider, spin, make lace, and play a musical instrument."[12]

At the outset, Teresa was desperately unhappy at Our Lady of Grace. It was not so much that she disliked the convent, but rather she suspected that her father had sent her away to protect her from the company of her cousins and to discourage her from the frivolous lifestyle that was so attractive to her. She was right, of course. Her unhappiness faded quickly though, because she was welcomed with open arms: "All were very pleased with me, for the Lord gave me the grace to be pleasing wherever I went, and so I was much loved. And though at that time I was strongly against becoming a nun, it made me happy to see such good nuns, for there were many good ones in that house, very modest, religious and circumspect."[13]

Even though her old friends tried to smuggle messages to her in an effort to distract her, she soon found herself happier at the convent than she had been at home. In the dormitory where the girls slept, there was a nun, Doña María Briceño, who proved to be a steadying influence for the teenage Teresa. She spent time with her and spoke to her about the things of God, and in doing so, she drew Teresa close to her.

Eventually, Teresa began to turn away from her bad habits and her worldly desires, but she still struggled with an inner resentment toward the religious life. She begged others to pray for her, so that she might come to accept God's will for her. Looking back on this time in her life, Teresa wrote: "This good company began to help me get rid of the habits that the bad company had caused and to turn my mind to the desire for eternal things and for some freedom from the antagonism that I felt within myself toward becoming a nun."[14]

For months, Teresa battled competing voices within herself that pitted the life of a married woman against that of a consecrated woman within the Church. While she had no enthusiasm for becoming a nun, marriage equally terrified her. She remembered her mother living in total submission to her father, and then dying young after so many years of childbearing. The ongoing conflict within herself ultimately affected not only her mental and emotional state, but her physical health, as well. This marked the beginning of a life plagued by severe illness in one form or another. Teresa endured these sufferings for the rest of her life, and some might say that keeping her at the foot of the cross was God's way of drawing her to himself.

The harshness of this first illness required that Teresa leave school and return to her father's home to rest and recuperate. When her health began to improve, she looked forward to spending time with her sister Maria, who lived in a nearby village. On the way to this happy destination, she stopped to spend a few days with her uncle, Don Pedro Sanchez de Cepeda. Don Pedro was a widower who was waiting until his son was raised before joining a monastery. Until then, he resided in his family home, where he immersed himself in religious books and private devotions.

Enjoying time with this kind and learned man sparked something in young Teresa. Being of an impressionable age and having struggled so long from various illnesses, Teresa opened herself up to the things of heaven. She began to see just how far she was from any kind of holiness, and she feared for the salvation of her soul. This seemingly insignificant experience in Saint Teresa's life proved to be a defining moment. Unknown to Teresa at the time, this introduction to a life of holiness would slowly change her forever.

Still, Teresa continued to wrestle with thoughts of both heaven and hell, and she feared for her future. In her autobiography, she speaks of this predicament: "Although my will did not completely incline [me] to being a nun, I saw that the religious life was the best and safest state, and so little by little I decided to force myself to accept it."[15]

Alonso was brokenhearted at the news of Teresa's intention to enter the convent. He refused his consent, but she was determined to go her own way. His response was a definite no: She could do what she wished after he died, but not before. Teresa, caught in the anguish of this battle, took her beloved brother Antonio (who later became a Dominican) into her confidence, and in secret they set out together on a November night. This time it was not to pursue a childish dream of martyrdom, but to begin her very personal way of the cross. She describes this as a pivotal event in her life:

> I remember, clearly and truly, that when I left my father's house, I felt that separation so keenly that the feeling will not be greater, I think, when I die. For it seemed that every bone in my body was being sundered. Since there was no love of God to take away my love for my father and relatives, everything so constrained me that if the Lord hadn't helped me, my reflections would not have been enough for me to continue on. In this situation, He gave me such courage against myself that I carried out the task.[16]

So ended Teresa's adolescence. The young woman of twenty-one made her decision, and she stuck by it. This was her first victory.

Reflection Questions

By spending so much time in conversation in the parlor, how is Teresa misusing her gift of teaching others or encouraging others in their spiritual growth? How can misusing the gifts that God gives us create havoc in our lives?

Everyone knows what it is like to be pulled in two directions, where God is on one side and our family and other obligations are on the other. How do you handle this? How does your current state of life play into this?

Teresa was in need of spiritual friendships and/or spiritual guidance. How important are these types of friendships, and how do they differ from regular friendships?

TERESA JOINS THE CARMELITES

With this decision behind her, Teresa saw her future clearly, and she began to move forward. Instead of joining the Convent of Our Lady of Grace, which she believed was too strict, she joined the Carmelite Convent of the Incarnation, which followed a modified Carmelite rule, allowing the nuns to entertain outside visitors in the parlor. After this monumental decision, Teresa was simply overcome with relief, energy, and joy. She had learned to face her fears, and they no longer had control over her. Never again did Teresa let fear prevent her from acting, especially where her love for God's will was concerned:

> As soon as I took the habit, the Lord gave me an understanding of how He favors those who use force with themselves to serve Him. No one noticed this struggle, but rather they thought I was very pleased. Within an

hour, He gave me such great happiness at being in the religious state of life that it never left me up to this day, and God changed the dryness my soul experienced into the greatest tenderness.

All the things of religious life delighted me, and it is true that sometimes while sweeping, during the hours that I used to spend in self-indulgence and self-adornment, I realized that I was free of all of that and experienced a new joy, which amazed me. And I couldn't understand where it came from.[17]

Despite the relief that she felt upon entering the convent, Teresa's character was slow to follow this change. She continued in her stubborn ways, and she refused to do anything that made her look foolish. This meant that she often balked under authority, and she was known to bristle at any form of correction, especially when it illuminated her lack of experience. Fortunately for everyone involved, her spirited nature did soften over time, and she became more serious when the gravity of the situation demanded it. She began to think for herself, and she started to learn the meaning of patience and self-sacrifice by observing these fundamental virtues in others:

There was a nun at the time afflicted with the most serious and painful illness, because there were some holes in her abdomen, which caused obstructions in such a way that she had to eject through them what she ate. She soon died from this. I observed that all feared that affliction. As for myself, I envied her patience. I asked God that, dealing with me in like manner, He would give me the illnesses by which he would be served.[18]

For the first year of her postulancy, Teresa's responsibilities were consistent with her social standing, in that she was not responsible for the menial tasks that the poorer, less fortunate nuns were expected to do.[19] Her life was pleasant, her companions were likable, and she did not have to do anything excessive in the way of penance or mortification. The Carmelite monasteries in Spain at that time did not observe the enclosure, in which the nuns have little contact with the outside world. Instead, there was always plenty of company on hand. Some two hundred persons, including servants and relatives, were living together at the monastery during Teresa's time there.

In many ways, Teresa's everyday life was seemingly unchanged. This fact sparked a period of questioning and restlessness, which left her wondering if she was really choosing God over the things of the world. Did she simply break "free of home and family just to find another equally pleasant and congenial environment behind the honey colored walls of the Incarnation?"[20] Or was something more required of her in order to grow in the life of the Spirit? Despite this inner struggle, Teresa stayed the course, and at the end of her first year, she made her vows with great resolution; now she was bound to Christ forever.

Her joy was short-lived, however, as Teresa once again fell seriously ill, scarcely a year after professing her solemn vows. This time she nearly died, and in fact, preparations for her funeral were underway when she unexpectedly awoke from a coma. Even though she had settled into life at the convent, she attributed this ailment to the change in food and lifestyle in her new surroundings, but again it seemed that God was calling her to go deeper into her faith and to grow closer to him. Her fainting spells and chest pains frightened those who witnessed them. Ever her loving father, Alonso, who had reconciled with Teresa shortly after she entered the convent, arranged for the best doctors in Ávila to treat her, but to no avail. He then sent her to a local "healer," who made everything so much worse. She nearly died before she was finally diagnosed with tuberculosis.[21] She reflects on her excruciating pain in the *Book of Her Life*:

> I suffered from a [paralysis] in which I remained for four days or a little less, without any feeling. … Only the Lord can know the unbearable torments I suffered within myself: my tongue bitten to pieces; my throat unable to let even water pass down … everything seeming to be disjointed; the greatest confusion in my head; all shriveled and drawn together in a ball. … I was unable to stir, not an arm or a foot, neither hand nor head, unable to move as though I were dead; only one finger on my right hand it seems I was able to move. Since there was no way of touching me, because I was so bruised that I couldn't endure it, they moved me about in a sheet, one of the nuns at one end and another at the other.[22]

By God's grace and infinite mercy, Teresa lived through this ordeal and consequently, we have the gift of her presence and knowledge even today. Even though it took nearly three years for her to totally recover from paralysis, she tells us that "when I began to go about on hands and knees, I praised God."[23] With this perspective of gratitude, she prayed to Saint Joseph, asking him to intercede for her, and she attributed her ability to rise and walk again to his intercession.[24] It is worth noting that devotion to Saint Joseph was a hallmark of Saint Teresa's life, and most of her foundations of reform bear his name.

It is impossible to exaggerate the importance of suffering in the life of Saint Teresa of Ávila. In fact, she never expected to live a long life, as pain and suffering were her constant companions. There are no medical records to determine the exact nature of her ailments, but from her writings and from her early biographers, a long list emerges. If we are to believe them, she suffered at various times from tuberculosis, heart disease, palsy, paralysis, trembling, epilepsy, sore throats, headaches, malaria, and fainting fits, among other things.[25]

Prayer or the Parlor

Living through a near death experience is a profound event that affects people in a variety of ways. Some turn to God, recognizing that life is a gift from him, and thus knowing him in a deep and intimate way becomes their main concern. Others recognize that life is short and because of this, they are determined to invest all of their energies in the people around them. After a stunning recovery from her near-death experience, Teresa found herself caught between these two ways of responding to the suffering she had endured. Should she devote herself totally to God in solitude and silence, reviving her early passion and love for prayer? Or should she throw herself wholeheartedly into visitations in the parlor, where she could spend her time encouraging others in their own spiritual pursuits?

For several decades, Teresa was absorbed in this battle between devotion to God and devotion to family and friends. Time and again, her desire for spiritual progress conflicted with her vivacious personality and her determination to create change in others. A lover of good conversation and lively debates, Saint Teresa wanted to transform the easy life in the parlor of the Incarnation, where family and friends frequently came and went, from a den of gossip and superficiality to a place of serious discussion and self-improvement. And in spite of her detractors, Teresa initiated discussions about prayer, and specifically how to pray. She was eager to talk not just about vocal prayer, but also mental prayer, prayer from the heart.

Over time, Teresa's relatives and friends gathered to hear her talk about the things of prayer. She specifically spoke to them about prayerful meditation based on the writings of a Spanish

Franciscan monk, Francisco de Osuna. In his book, Third Spiritual Alphabet, the Franciscan introduces his audience to the "prayer of recollection." This prayer simply encourages the soul to gather together its various faculties, in order to concentrate the mind and the will on God alone, while letting everything else go. It consists in the realization that God is in me, and my soul is his temple. "The basic value of recollection consists not in how well we can think of Him, but rather, in how well we can love Him."[26] Later in her life, Teresa recalled that before reading this book by Francisco de Osuna, "I did not know how to proceed in prayer or how to be recollected. And so, I was very happy with this book and resolved to follow [this] path with all my strength."[27]

One of her first disciples in this "school" of prayer was Alonso, her rapidly aging father. As Alonso approached the end of his life, he was looking for spiritual answers and consolations. Just thinking about heaven and hell gave him the determination to secure a place in the former, rather than the latter. For this reason, he frequently visited the parlor to hear Teresa speak on the subject of prayer, and he humbly followed his daughter's instructions. And then something happened. Teresa's father came to the stark realization that merely talking about prayer was a serious waste of time. He would rather spend time praying than frequenting Teresa's parlor. He may have also sensed that while his daughter could speak eloquently about the prayer of recollection, she herself lacked the discipline and the will to simply pray.

His intuition turned out to be right on target. Teresa was very skilled in talking about prayer, but she later admitted that there were too many instances in which she excused herself from practicing it. She was partaking in the sacraments, but her spirit was dry and desolate.

She innately knew that the Lord was sending her many spiritual graces, and because of this, she wanted to pass her good fortune on to others by encouraging them to pray. However, in this undertaking she was very much at the mercy of her emotions, lacking in discretion and self-discipline. Teresa was clearly in need of guidance and support. Lack of education, training, and experience, together with a larger-than-life personality, had placed her in danger of self-reliance and error.

The Carmel of the Incarnation simply did not provide the structure and support that Teresa sorely needed. In this setting, serious or prolonged solitude and reflection seemed out of the question. During this time of internal conflict, Teresa made many worthy resolutions, but they were not strong enough to keep her from falling into occasions of offending God. By her own admission, she experienced a deep spiritual weariness. Essentially, her soul was tired.[28] She was going "from pastime to pastime, from vanity to vanity, from one occasion to another,"[29] and in doing so, she was becoming more and more conflicted.

In the meantime, her relationship with her father was deteriorating. Even though it hurt her deeply, she deceived him into believing that she had stopped praying because of her health, claiming that it was all she could do to keep up with her choir duties. No doubt, this caused him great pain. In fact, we have to wonder what made him sadder — that his daughter was too ill to pray, or for reasons that he could not fully understand, her inner state of mind made it impossible.

While Alonso and Teresa were living in this unsatisfactory state, he became seriously ill. Trying to conceal her grief, Teresa went home to care for him. For three days, he went in and out of consciousness, waking only on the day of his death, Christmas Eve 1543. Halfway through citing the Creed, Teresa tells us that he died, "looking like an angel."[30] In losing her father, she lost the person who was dearest to her. Similar to when she joined the convent, she felt as if her very soul was being torn from her:

I suffered much hardship during his sickness. I believed
I served him somewhat for the trials he suffered during
mine. Although I was very sick, I forced myself. Since in
losing him, I was losing every good and joy, and he was
everything to me, I had great determination not to show
him my grief and until he would die to act as though I
were well. When I saw him coming to the end of his life,
it seemed my soul was being wrenched from me, for I
loved him dearly.[31]

As her father lay dying, he invited each of his children to come
look at him, so they could see how quickly he had reached his
last day. He wanted to remind them that all things on earth pass
away, and that eternity is to be found in God alone. Nothing else
matters. His words had a lasting impact on Teresa. Her conviction of the passing nature of life on earth, her sensitivity, and her
feeling of emptiness all helped to create a vacuum in her soul
that could only be filled by God.[32]

In the aftermath of her sorrow, she bared her soul to her
father's confessor, a Dominican priest and a very learned man.[33]
He encouraged her to go to Communion regularly and to resume the practice of prayer. This she did, and she never again
stopped praying, although she continued to struggle in trying to
amend her life. She had periods of backsliding, weariness, and
many times, she was tempted to give up. For whatever reason,
she simply could not integrate the spiritual and social sides of
her nature, no matter how hard she tried. At thirty-nine, Saint
Teresa was well into her adult life, having been a religious sister
for nearly two decades. She now found herself at a crossroads,
and though it was unclear to her at the time, God was once again
about to change her life forever.

Teresa's Conversion

Teresa's life-changing experience happened one day in 1554 as she entered the oratory at the convent. When she arrived at the chapel, she saw a bust of the wounded Christ.[34] Being a true representation of Spanish devotional art, this statue captured the bloody realism and brutality of Jesus' suffering. Gazing at the face of her Savior, Saint Teresa was overwhelmed by the sense of her own sinfulness:

> It happened to me that one day entering the oratory I saw a statue they had borrowed for a certain feast to be celebrated in the house. It represented the much-wounded Christ and was very devotional so that beholding it I was utterly distressed in seeing Him that way, for it well represented what He suffered for us. … I threw myself down before Him with the greatest outpouring of tears.[35]

Continuing this thought, she explained:

> I think I then said that I would not rise from there until He granted what I was begging Him for. I believe certainly this was beneficial to me, because from that time I went on improving.[36]

This was the moment of Teresa's *fiat*, the moment of her "yes," the moment when she finally gave herself entirely to Christ. For Teresa, this moment began a new way of living here on earth. While she was still a step away from resolving her problems over personal relationships, there was no longer any doubt that God was at last the center of her life. She was forever "as wax imprinted with God's seal."[37]

This experience launched Teresa into a period of serious conversion, a period of intensified prayer, recollection, and reading. Because she had no close spiritual confidants and no confessor to guide her, she turned to the great spiritual writers of the past for help. She found a soulmate in Saint Augustine. In reading the account of his conversion, Teresa admitted: "When I came to the passage where he speaks about his conversion and read how he heard that voice in the garden, it only seemed to me, according to what I felt in my heart, that it was I the Lord called. I remained for a long time totally dissolved in tears and feeling within myself utter distress and weariness."[38] From that point on, she was firm in her resolve, and even though she continued to navigate stormy seas, the vacillation and uncertainty were finally over.

Sixteenth-Century Monasteries, Religious Life, and Reform

Throughout the history of Christianity, there have always been those who make the decision to leave their families and live together in communities not of blood, but of faith. These communities range from loosely organized households of lay people who are free to leave at any time, to those that are well defined and ordered around a rule of life. These ordered communities include monasteries or convents of men and women who take vows, in which they permanently consecrate themselves to religious life. Regrettably, during Saint Teresa's time, the monasteries were suffering from all manner of abuses stemming from the abandonment of their original rule of life. The three fundamental principles of monastic life — poverty, chastity, and obedience, known as the evangelical counsels — were cast aside for wealth, promiscuity, and power. Many of those in monasteries did not even have a genuine vocation.

For example, some women entered a monastery because they lacked an offer for marriage and/or they had no dowry to bring to a marriage. In some cases, the women who entered were widows seeking stability in community life. Added to this were the limited social opportunities available for women. Likewise, some of the men entering religious life did so as a last resort or to escape misfortune, rather than to seek a life of holiness. Alas, there was little to distinguish these monastic communities from the society at large. Without a clear grasp of the vow of poverty, both men and women fell prey to possessiveness and materialism, which fostered a kind of class structure in the community. The idea of the "haves" and the "have-nots" increased when things such as a place at the table, a private room, or adornments of dress were at stake. This was exactly Teresa's situation at the Convent of the Incarnation. To continue to grow interiorly, she knew she must detach from these unnecessary privileges.

Consequently, after her conversion, Teresa's friendships were entirely God-centered. This focus gave her the strength and conviction to disengage from the people who wanted to draw her into a mediocre existence. Over time, her life began to blossom in holiness, steadfastness in prayer, and love for others. It was as if she was seeing things for the first time. Christ was clearly forming Teresa into his likeness, and she could not hide this transformation, nor did she want to. Indeed, she was on the verge of discovering her "vocation within a vocation." Although she was unaware of it at the time, God was preparing her to reform the Carmelite Order and to establish new houses of prayer.

Once Teresa fully abandoned herself to Christ, an abundance of graces came very quickly in the form of locutions, visions, and raptures. She entered what is known as the mystical life, in which she spent much of her time in a state of contemplation, reflecting on God. While in this mystical state, God was present to her without any effort or intensity of devotion on her part. This profound grace allowed Teresa to see the world in its totality. For her, there were no barriers between our humanity and God's divinity. During such times, Saint Teresa's worldview encompassed everything, including heaven, hell, purgatory, saints, devils, and the like. Likewise, she began to "hear" Christ speaking to her interiorly, and she "saw" his hands, his face, and his resurrected body in all its glory.[39] In Teresa's own words:

> The Lord almost always showed Himself to me as risen, also when He appeared in the Host — except at times when He showed me his wounds in order to encourage me when I was suffering tribulation. Sometimes He appeared on the cross or in the garden, and a few times with the crown of thorns; sometimes He also appeared carrying the cross on account of my needs and the needs of others. But His body was always glorified.[40]

Perhaps the most well-known mystical occurrence from the life of Saint Teresa was her "Transverberation of the Heart," which occurred in 1560. Teresa explained that in this intense and overpowering moment, she was aware that an angel pierced her heart with a golden dart tipped with the fire of God's love. According to Teresa, the arrow was plunged into her breast, causing excruciating pain and unspeakable joy. Remarkably, when Teresa's heart was removed after her death, it was not only incorrupt, but it was also marked by a small hole.[41]

Now that she was in the midst of this extraordinary journey into the unknown realms of spiritual depth, God saw fit to send Saint Teresa an army of confessors and spiritual persons to help guide her. Over the years, she had roughly twenty-five different confessors and directors, most of whom were from the Jesuit order. Three of her confessors, Peter of Alcantara, Francis Borgia, and John of the Cross, are now saints themselves. And it was a Dominican priest, Garcia de Toledo, who first encouraged Teresa to write down the details of her life. Because Teresa was initially uncertain and terrified because she did not know if her visions were coming from the Holy Spirit or from the Father of Lies, she sought direction at every stage and from every quarter. In fact, the fabric of Saint Teresa's mystical life, and her development in the art of prayer, is inextricably tied to her confessors.[42]

Reflection Questions

Teresa spent years in a state of flux primarily because she believed that it was within her power to change. Later in her life, Teresa claimed that self-reliance was what nearly destroyed her. Practically speaking, how does self-reliance get in our way?

Does poverty only have to do with the lack of material things? What is the essence of spiritual poverty?

THE REFORM OF THE CARMELITES

As life would have it, one September evening in 1560, Teresa, her two nieces, and some other companions were engaged in conversation about the Church, the way of prayer, the new religious orders being founded, and the old ones being reformed. Invariably, their favorite topic came up, which was the need for more solitude, as well as their desire for a new style of monastic life. One of Teresa's nieces, a young nun, chimed in with the suggestion: "All right then, let's all go and start another kind of life, something more solitary like the hermits had."[43]

Most of those present took her comment in stride, but Teresa could not dismiss it so lightly. Seeing this, the others encouraged her to accept the challenge of founding a new convent based on the primitive rule[44] of the early Carmelites. She was stunned. Certainly, she had spent plenty of time trying to reform herself, but never once had she thought of herself in the role of reformer! Not only that, there was also the drawback of her age and lack of revenue. How and where would she start such a venture?

God came to Teresa's aid in the person of Guiomar de Ulloa, a widowed friend who offered both moral support and financial aid. Meanwhile, the younger women involved were burning with enthusiasm and ready to begin this holy work. Tempered by age and experience, Teresa cautioned them and instructed them to take these ideas to God in prayer, assuring them that she would do the same. Little by little, as the days passed, she became convinced that the Lord was asking her to start a new monastery under the primitive rule.[45] In his book *The 35 Doctors of the Church*, Father Christopher Rengers, OFM Cap, described Teresa's transformation as one of total submission. Up until now,

> Teresa's story is one of struggle toward spiritual maturity. Pain and infirmity of the body, anguish of mind, restlessness that sought both solitude and companionship (she keenly needed both), the co-existence of remarkable mystical experiences with faults and a certain lack of mortification: all entered into her growth.
>
> But eventually she reached a peaceful synthesis, and she was ready for her great work of reform of the Carmelite Order. While carrying out this reform, her soul would continue to grow to spiritual maturity, she would compose her writings, and she would attain a more complete and uninterrupted union with God.[46]

Ultimately, "Madre" Teresa could do nothing but "bow before the providence of circumstances."[47] With a renewed sense of purpose and God-given zeal, thirty-nine-year-old Teresa daydreamed about what this new monastery might look like. First, she envisioned a small convent that was limited to thirteen sisters. Second, and most importantly, this intimate group of women would keep strict enclosure and focus their day around prayer. Teresa's nuns would also learn to work for a living, and they would celebrate a simple liturgy, in contrast to the elaborate liturgies of the larger communities. Additionally, it was Teresa's desire for the nuns to live in poverty, enjoying a common life lived in friendship with Christ and with each other. As she put it: "In this house where there are no more than thirteen — nor must there be any more — all must be friends, all must be loved, all must be held dear, all must be helped."[48]

Saint Teresa's intentions were clear and well-defined. Her desire was to give her nuns the opportunity not only to lead a life of prayer, but to do it in a serious way, actively fighting the errors of the time and sacrificing for the salvation of souls. She expected that they would be trained in various careers, as administrators, scribes, accountants, pharmacists, and teachers, as all were needed in this new community of devout souls. She also insisted that her nuns learn to read, for Teresa's new Carmel would be "a friend of books, of learning, of verses, and the canticles of St. John of the Cross."[49]

Despite the fact that she had no house, no real money, and no official permission to proceed, Teresa energetically set about making preparations, because she was confident that God would lead her. Although she was first and foremost a woman of prayer, she easily adapted to her new responsibilities by developing facets of her personality that were in many ways unknown to her. This role required that she be a leader and an administrator, a breadwinner and a mother. She had to concern herself with the nitty-gritty details of life, while at the same time, she had to fulfill the obligations that were required by her superiors in Rome.

Teresa proved that she was up to the task. She was able to be fully present to both God and to the business at hand, depending on what each new circumstance required. She was indeed a woman of prayer and a woman of action, as evidenced by her simple and profound motto: "Do what you are doing."[50] In other words, she believed that we must be fully present to the task before us, no matter if we are in the priory or the pew. In her book, *The Way of Perfection*, Saint Teresa wrote: "A true contemplative lives in the present with all of its ambiguities and not in some far-away realm of perfection."[51] As a true contemplative who was also a foundress, Teresa was able to manage the inner world of the spirit and the outside world of rules and responsibilities.

She was authentically a "woman's woman" in her tenderness and her desire to love and be loved. In hundreds of little ways, she demonstrated her great sensitivity and affection for others, her care and concern for children, and her commitment to her family. However, perhaps the most significant aspect of her motherly heart was her devotion to and love for the religious women in her care. Teresa frequently spoke of the crushing loneliness she experienced when she was away from her sisters, as well as the anxiety she felt as she led them into the uncharted waters of a new foundation, knowing and not knowing the hardships ahead.

No matter how you look at it (literally or figuratively), the road ahead was never going to be easy. As the Mother Superior, she got her first taste of this new challenge when she sought approval from the hierarchy of the very Church that was in desperate need of reform. The initial steps of this journey began, as they should, in the context of spiritual direction. Knowing the proper order of her responsibilities, Teresa first presented her idea for the formation of a new convent to her Jesuit confessor, Father Balthazar Alvarez, who in turn sent her to the Carmelite Provincial, Father Angel de Salazar. Upon hearing of Teresa's plan, Father Angel gave her his blessing and permission to proceed.

With that stumbling block out of the way, Teresa's friend Guiomar de Ulloa began to look for a house that would be suitable for the new monastery. As these inquiries became common knowledge, the townsfolk rose up in protest, and as a result, pandemonium ensued. Both Teresa and Guiomar were mercilessly persecuted. Why does the city need another convent? Who will support them? How will the nuns live? Who is this Teresa de Ahumada anyway? Did her visions make her crazy?

Alarmed by the public's reaction, Father Angel withdrew his approval. This decision was confirmed by the storm of indignation that swept through the Carmel of the Incarnation when the nuns learned of Teresa's intentions to leave and to found another convent. It was no surprise that they viewed her dream as a direct criticism of their lifestyle and a rejection of all that they held dear. She explained this situation in her autobiography:

> I was very much disliked throughout my monastery because I had wanted to found a more enclosed monastery. They said I was insulting them, that in this monastery I could also serve God since there were others in it better than I, that I had no love for the house; that it would be better to procure income for this place rather than some other. ... Yet, since I couldn't mention the main factor, which is that the Lord had commanded me to do this, I didn't know how to act; so I remained silent.[52]

In a different place, she writes:

> I didn't know what to do; it seemed to me that [the
> nuns] were partly right. While weary and recommend-
> ing myself to God, His Majesty began to console and en-
> courage me. He told me that in this I would see what the
> saints who had founded religious orders had suffered,
> that I would have to suffer much more persecution than
> I could imagine and that we shouldn't let it bother us.[53]

Taking Our Lord at his word, Saint Teresa returned to the task
before her. Over the next several months, she fulfilled her duties at the Incarnation without incident. She devoted this time
of waiting to long periods of silence, intense prayer, and fasting.
The most pressing issue was to secure a piece of property in Ávila, without incurring the wrath of the townspeople. Finding a
somewhat "hidden" solution to the problem, she slyly arranged
for her sister, Juana, to purchase a house, under the pretense that
it was for her and her husband. In due time, however, it became
the convent of Teresa's dreams.

All told, it took two years, from 1560 to 1562, to plan and
finalize her first foundation, Saint Joseph's of Ávila. In the midst
of this, Father Angel sent Teresa to Toledo to stay at the home of
a very wealthy and noble lady, Luisa de la Cerda, who was griev-
ing the recent death of her husband. Luisa knew of Teresa and of
the power of her prayers, and she had persuaded Father Angel
to send Teresa to console her. With this assignment, he was able
to get Teresa out of the commotion in Ávila, and send comfort
to Luisa, as well.

Having no other choice, Teresa agreed to go. In January
1562, after a long and brutally cold trip, she arrived in Toledo,
the city of her ancestors. She was pleasantly surprised to find
in Luisa de la Cerda a woman of faith who was deeply in love

with God, an ideal hostess, and a fast friend. The two women found comfort in each other. Teresa entered into Luisa's world of Spanish high society as naturally as if she was born into it. Living with Luisa provided her the opportunity to rub shoulders with all kinds of people from all levels of society and all walks of life. Among them were bankers, muleteers, merchants, boatmen, beggars, bishops, sacristans, theologians, dukes and duchesses, princes and princesses, and even a king and a queen. Many of them became Teresa's friends and benefactors.

By being her usual, unflappable self, Teresa was a godsend, not only to Luisa, but to everyone she met. Underneath it all, however, she believed it was unjust to insist on titles and "honor" when we all share in a common humanity. She always maintained that this fanfare held no special appeal for her, a fact that she shared in her autobiography:

> I learned how little regard ought to be paid to rank, and how, the higher the rank, the greater are the trials and cares it brings with it. And I learned that people of rank have to behave according to their state, which hardly allows them to live ... often the very food they eat has more to do with their position than their liking. So it was that I came to hate the very desire to be a great lady. God deliver me from this sinful fuss.[54]

While Teresa was a blessing to the people she befriended in Toledo, the time she spent in Toledo was also a blessing to Teresa. Here at last she found peace in her soul, a direct result of the hours she spent in silence and prayer. Over the course of these months, Teresa had the opportunity to finish the first rendition of her autobiography, *The Book of Her Life*. In this book, she tells us that while in Toledo, the Lord granted her the most wonderful [spiritual] favors.[55] In fact, wearing her threadbare habit in the marbled halls of the Cerda home caused Teresa to reflect that, up until now, she had trusted the world much more than she had ever trusted God. She was now at the point in her life where she understood that "the true remedy against a fall is to be attached to a cross and trust in Him who placed Himself upon it. ... He is the true friend."[56] With this, her spiritual apprenticeship was complete. She was ready to begin the real mission of her life.

In June 1562, Father Angel reached out to Teresa, telling her that she could stay in the relative quiet of Toledo, or she could return to Ávila. She knew that her work in Toledo was finished, but she was not eager to go back to Ávila, fearing what awaited her. Nevertheless, she summoned her courage and returned to the battle. Once she arrived in her native city after a hot and dusty journey, Saint Teresa went directly to the Incarnation, reported to her superiors, and slipped quietly back into the measured routine of the community. Unbeknownst to her, her dream was about to come true. Teresa's hour was at hand.

The very night that Teresa arrived in Ávila, her longtime companion, Guiomar de Ulloa, received the necessary paperwork from Rome authorizing the new foundation. Shortly thereafter, the bishop of Ávila, who was initially resistant toward Teresa's idea of reform, announced that after meeting Teresa, he was willing to oversee the foundation, rather than have it fall under the jurisdiction of the Carmelite fathers. William T. Walsh, one of Teresa's biographers, wrote that "[the bishop] agreed to take her monastery under his protection and jurisdiction and from that day on, he was her loyal and unflinching friend until he died, requesting in his will that he be buried beside her."[57]

The new monastery opened on August 24, 1562, on the feast of Saint Bartholomew. It was no accident that this new endeavor was given over to the protection of this worthy apostle, who was known for his defense against the wiles and assaults of the devil. On this day, Madre Teresa presented her four hand-picked novices to the bishop's representative, Father Gaspar Daza, ironically one of her early detractors. In this humble abode that Juana purchased for Teresa, Father Daza offered Mass and enthroned the Blessed Sacrament, where it remained for several centuries. As Teresa watched her four novices receive their religious names and become officially cloistered, she was reminded of the prayers of so many days and nights, which in God's time, he now answered and fulfilled. "It was a glorious moment for [her] as she fell on her knees before the altar, and became so utterly lost in prayer that three or four hours passed before she returned to her senses."[58]

Legend has it that prior to moving in to the new monastery, Teresa removed her shoes and walked barefoot "to the crypt of the beautiful old church of San Vincente, just outside [Ávila's] city walls, a building she would have seen daily from the Convent of the Incarnation. There she lit a candle before the shrine of the Virgin de la Soterrana and dedicated herself and her work to the service of Christ and his mother." [59] From that moment on, she no longer called herself Doña Teresa de Cepeda y Ahumada.[60] Rather, she was now "Teresa of Jesus."[61] This name change reflected the profound conversion taking place in her heart. Her new way of life spoke of "poverty, silence, and simplicity, of austerity and mortification, of solitude, prayer, and love."[62]

Her heavy wool habit, white cloak, and sandals all symbolized this new life of asceticism. The simple furnishings of the new monastery also articulated this interior change in Teresa. Still today, we can see the "brick floors and narrow cells furnished only with a bed, a cork mat, and a crucifix"[63] in the rooms of Saint Joseph's. As prioress, Teresa afforded herself a "simple stool with no back, no arms, and no comfort or unnecessary decoration,"[64] once again confirming the humility of this great saint.

Saint Joseph's was small, but it was big enough for Teresa's new community of cloistered nuns. They lived as a close-knit family and spent most of their day in solitude. They prayed, read spiritual books, and did much of their work in the quiet of their cells. They also met for the liturgy, for brief periods of recreation, and for frugal meals. She used to say that "God walks among the pots and pans as well as anywhere else." [65] At long last, Saint Teresa was able to live the life she longed for and for which she had fought so hard. Saint Joseph's was her little "heaven on earth,"[66] and for five wonderful years, she enjoyed the most restful time of her life.[67]

Reflection Questions

Why it is important to have a structure within a religious community regarding not only the time for prayer, but also administrative tasks, fundraising, and even the materials for the habit?

What does the reaction of the nuns at the Incarnation to Teresa's plans tell us about human nature? Similarly, Father Angel de Salazar withdraws his support of the monastery based on the reactions and opinions of others. Does this also say something about human nature?

MANDATE TO WRITE

Like so many things in Teresa's life, she never planned or intended to write spiritual books. It was only out of humble obedience to her superiors and confessors that she agreed to do so, but not without a bit of complaining, as evidenced in this conversation with one of her spiritual directors:

> Why do they wish me to write? Let the theologians do it. They have studied, and I am only a simpleton. What do you want me to say? I shall put one word instead of

the other and so do harm. There are plenty of books on prayer already. For the love of God, let me go on with my spinning, go to choir, and follow the Rule like the other Sisters; I am not made to write; I have neither the health nor the intelligence for it.[68]

This directive was given to Teresa during a time in Spain when it was rare for a woman to be educated enough to write, but she was fortunate to have received a kind of homeschooling from her parents. In her writing, she combined her human qualities with her divine gifts to convey to others what it means to be open to the depths of an authentic spiritual life. In fact, some say that Saint Teresa is perhaps the greatest woman ever to handle a pen.

Saint Teresa uses a simple and direct style in her writings. She writes without pretense in the common everyday language of the Spanish people. With an intensely practical mind, she expresses her ideas in such a way that her readers can understand them and put them into practice. Whether it is a letter to a family friend or a treatise on prayer, Teresa writes in the same characteristic style, with a passion for exactness and precision. She writes as she speaks, anxious to say everything at once, yet the material is presented in clear, sharp, and vibrant tones.

Still human and not without shortcomings, Saint Teresa insisted that her writing be taken "as is." Without the patience and time required for mechanics, she refused to correct or change what she had written once her thoughts were on paper. Because of this personal eccentricity, there is a repetitive quality in some of her writings. In her writings, Teresa often comments on this dilemma, wondering if she has already said what she is saying currently. Knowing this, it helps to remember that she often wrote late into the night when her head was "making noises" and she was cold and exhausted.

Teresa's ability to see things in reality and to keep them in the right perspective helps to explain her ever present sense of humor and her keen, penetrating understanding of those around her. Perhaps her humor is her most endearing quality. Very likely, she is one of the "funniest" saints to hold a place among the Doctors of the Church. By using quips, adages, and ironic complaints in a non-threatening way to inspire and amuse us, Teresa proves that the absurdities of life do not have to defeat us. Furthermore, she suggests that there is a connection between humor and our spiritual life, which is especially relevant to our contemporary journey. It reveals a certain humility, another essential in the spiritual life. To be sure, Teresa believed that we must take God and the Gospel seriously, but we should not take ourselves too seriously. A perfect illustration of this is the story of the time Teresa was traveling to one of her convents, when she was knocked off her donkey. She fell into the mud and injured her leg. When she asked God about this mishap, he responded by telling her that this is how he treats his friends, to which she replied: "That is why you have so few of them."[69]

For the most part, Teresa's writings are autobiographical, and they spring from the depth of her prayer and contemplation. Her vivid imagination notices everything, forgets nothing, and is always overflowing with ideas. With her amazing capacity to see and utilize analogies and metaphors, she brings the complexities of the spiritual life within reach of those just beginning their spiritual journey. For example, in *The Book of Her Life*, she writes with disarming simplicity, explaining the stages in the life of prayer through her famous analogy of "four ways of watering a garden." The use of water as a metaphor for the stages of prayer is a classic example of Saint Teresa's writing style. It is also a metaphor that is particularly appropriate for those who live on the severe, dry Castilian plains. These simple folks are well acquainted with the importance of water and the difficulty of providing enough of it to soak their gardens.

Using this analogy, Teresa compares a beginner in prayer to a gardener as she explains that the first way of watering a garden is by means of a well. This method is the most laborious because drawing water from a well takes a lot of effort on the part of the gardener (the beginner in prayer). According to Teresa, using a bucket to draw water from a well is similar to the way we start to pray. We come to prayer because we are aware of our dry souls and our need of the living waters of Christ. However, it takes a lot of effort, because keeping the senses recollected is very tiring. Because they are used to a life of distraction, beginners have to accustom themselves to pay no attention to what they see or hear, and this can be challenging. Consequently, the first stage of prayer is marked by our actions, and most often, perseverance is needed.

After this beginning stage, prayer gets easier. It does not require as much effort. To illustrate this, Teresa uses the image of an aqueduct, which brings water from the mountains, flowing into our lives. In this scenario, the gardener is able to draw more water with less labor, which allows for some rest, instead of being continuously at work. We experience comfort, security, and confidence knowing that the flow of fresh water from faraway heights is coming to us in an unending current of living water. Still, it is inevitable that dryness will come, and weeds will continue to grow in our garden. Teresa acknowledges that "there is no state of prayer so lofty that it will not be necessary to return many times to the beginning."[70] Christ's call to discipleship demands self-denial and the willingness to humbly carry our cross and follow him. The depth of our prayer life depends upon it, and Saint Teresa shows us that there is no other path to happiness.

Teresa uses the image of a flowing stream to explain the third stage of prayer. In this image, we benefit from the running water, which requires little effort from us. She uses this comparison to introduce us to the divine favors of prayer, which are beyond what any human effort can obtain or merit. Here we access the "fountain of living water" that God provides to us through his unending grace. While we are experiencing this third stage of prayer, it is a perfect time to use our energies on behalf of God's kingdom. As we are resting in the endless stream of God's graces, we can use our creative energies to spread the Gospel, planting seeds everywhere we go.

Finally, Teresa uses the comforting idea of a gentle rain for the fourth stage of prayer. This stage exceeds all of the others in spiritual excellence. The person who experiences this type of prayer is often referred to as a mystic and is one who is blessed with an enduring union with God. In this most perfect expression of prayer, God gives this person a virtual downpour of rain. He supernaturally soaks the garden!

The simple act of watering a garden is just one of the metaphors that Saint Teresa uses to teach us about progressing in the life of prayer. She knows of what she speaks, particularly when it comes to discussing the art of prayer or lack thereof. In her autobiography, she shares that in the beginning "she never dared to begin prayer without a book,"[71] and even then, there were times when she would just stare at the clock, wishing that her hour was over. But she persevered, and in the following passage she encourages us not to miss so great an opportunity:

> Whoever has not begun the practice of prayer, I beg for the love of God not to go without so great a good. There is nothing here to fear, but only something to desire. … And if one perseveres, I trust then in the mercy of God, who never fails to betray anyone who has taken Him for a friend. For mental prayer in my opinion is nothing else than an intimate sharing between friends; it means taking time to be alone with Him who we know loves us.[72]

In reviewing Teresa's books, it is easy to see their spiritual significance and to understand Teresa's place among the Doctors of the Church. She wrote books of infinite worth, which emerged in the midst of countless interruptions and were often penned in the late hours of night.

Frequently writing with fingers frozen to the bone, Teresa wrote rapidly and with extraordinary ease, never changing a word, never looking back. Her four major works are: *The Book of Her Life*, completed in 1562; *The Way of Perfection*, probably written in 1566; *The Interior Castle*, composed in less than six months during 1577; and *The Book of Her Foundations*, completed in 1582, about two months before her death.

Books

The *Book of Her Life (Life)* is the first of Saint Teresa's works. It is one of the greatest spiritual autobiographies of all time, and it places Teresa among the small number of canonized saints who recount for us the intimate interactions between God and their souls. She refers to it as the "big book" or the "book of the Mercies of God."[73] With great charm and goodness, Saint Teresa recounts her early life as a child at home and at school. She tells the story of her vocation and the years of her personal struggle in the convent. It is here that Teresa shares the challenges of her physical ailments, and she gives us the particulars of her call to conversion and prayer. The chapters on prayer are the heart of the work, and they constitute a classic treatise on this subject. In a very real way, she pours herself into this book. In giving it to a friend to read, Teresa tells her: "Remember, it is my soul which I confide to you."[74]

Shortly after finishing *Life*, Teresa began *The Way of Perfection*, which is really two small books that she wrote for the benefit of the nuns in the monastery of Saint Joseph's in Ávila. Teresa refers to it as the "Little Book of the *Pater Noster*," and she writes it in the style of a dialogue between herself and her beloved sisters. The first book is an enthusiastic mandate to follow the evangelical counsels (poverty, chastity, and obedience) and to make "reparation for the sins of Catholics and fallen away heretics."[75] The second book is on the Our Father, and it explains prayer in its various forms and degrees. There are three chapters on the Holy Eucharist, which are "among the most beautiful and lyrical of all of her writings."[76]

The Book of the Foundations is Teresa's last book, and it is perhaps the most popular of all of her writings. She composed this book in the scanty intervals between great activity and unending distractions, and she completed it just a few months before her death. It reveals her character and temperament, her gaiety, courage, patience, and lightheartedness more fully than any of the others. She weaves colorful details into her accounts of establishing each of the foundations, including entering towns in secret and in the dead of night, lest a foundation be rejected before the Eucharist could be celebrated in the morning. Teresa and her companions navigate swollen rivers, sleep in vile inns, and travel in a covered wagon beneath the burning sun. While her total self-gift to the Lord and her advanced prayer are evident in the *Book of Foundations*, she also shares her feelings of fear, physical pain, and weariness. Despite this, her unmistakable gift of humor comes through loud and clear, as does her simple appreciation for the "little things" of life.

In between *The Way of Perfection* and the *Book of Foundations*, Saint Teresa wrote the pinnacle of all of her works, *The Interior Castle*. This spiritual classic describes the seven major stages of growth in prayer that lead to union with God. In this book, she depicts the soul as a castle that has many rooms. God dwells in the innermost room, which is at the interior depths of the human soul. Despite very poor health and the countless difficulties of founding new monasteries, Saint Teresa wrote this great work in just under six months. This manuscript is preserved in the Carmelite Monastery in Seville. To be sure, the writing of this masterpiece was not an easy task for Teresa, and she acknowledged as much in the prologue of the book:

> Not many things that I have been ordered to do under obedience have been as difficult for me as is this present task of writing about prayer. First, it doesn't seem the Lord is giving me either the spirit or the desire to undertake the work. Second, I have been experiencing now for three months such great noise and weakness in my head that I've found it a hardship even to write concerning necessary business matters.[77]

Teresa's written legacy also includes the Constitutions for her Carmelite Sisters, as well as "Spiritual Testimonies," soliloquies, poems, and a brief treatise, "On Making the Visitation," making Teresa one of the most prolific of the Doctors of the Church. To this day, we have the thoughts and words of this great saint to ponder, explore, and take to heart. Through her writings, we have access to both her remarkable life and the mystical experiences of her soul. Her writings tell us something else about Teresa. She was always looking forward, which is a true sign of hope. In her own way, she personified hope for everyone in general, but especially for her Carmelite sisters.

Letters

Saint Teresa was a born letter writer, and many people think that her letters are her most valuable work, in that they are the most faithful mirror of her mind and soul. As one author expresses it:

> [In her letters] she deals with all subjects, her gravest concerns, such as the defense of the Reform, and her daily preoccupations, such as ordering fowl for the com-

munity dinner. She writes, burdened as she always is, in haste, encroaching on her night's sleep, never, save most rarely, re-reading what she has written, and with that charming conversational ease in which she excelled.[78]

During her lifetime, she wrote about fifteen thousand letters, of which fewer than five hundred are preserved.[79] All of her letters were written in her distinct, firm, and well-defined handwriting on sheets of folded paper with "IHS"[80] at the top. She signed them with her religious name, "Teresa of Jesus." Only one preserved letter has her signature from her early days, "Doña Teresa de Ahumada." In God's providence, these letters found their way into every corner of Spain and even into the New World.

As a high-born Castilian lady, Teresa's letters have the ease and quiet distinction that reflect her refinement, culture, and good manners. In them, as in all of her social relations, she shows the unstudied courtesy of a lady of quality, from a country in which the Catholic Faith refined and elevated the manners of society. Her letters reveal a woman of great sensitivity and common sense, observant, tactful, distinctly humorous, and extraordinarily kind and sincere.

Reflection Questions

How does humor help us put things into perspective?

Teresa did not want to write, but she did so out of obedience to her superiors, and her books have become spiritual masterpieces. Think of a time you did something purely out of obedience. What did you learn from that experience?

TERESA'S LEGACY

At the age of fifty-two, after she had lived the life of a cloistered nun for thirty-two years, Saint Teresa's life took another unexpected turn. Sometime in August of 1566, she met Alonso Maldonado, a Franciscan Friar who was just returning from the West Indies. He told Teresa and the others about the many millions of souls who were perishing there for lack of Christian teaching.[81] He asked the nuns to do penance for those who were suffering. Upon hearing this, Teresa's heart began to stir, and she tells us that she was so grief-stricken over the loss of so many souls that she could not contain herself.[82] She longed to be of help.

Some six months after Maldonado's impassioned plea for help, the Carmelite General, Juan Bautista Rubeo, visited Ávila. This was an extraordinary event, since he lived in Rome and rarely traveled to Spain, and certainly not to Ávila. The trip, however, was not just a personal whim. Rather, the Carmelite General visited Spain at the invitation of the Spanish King, Philip II. Philip was anxious to reform all of the religious orders in Spain, as set forth by the Council of Trent. The very thought of encountering Father Rubeo struck a chord of fear in Teresa, for she expected him to be angry with her for placing Saint Joseph's under the jurisdiction of the local bishop, rather than under the Carmelite Order. Consequently, it came as a total surprise that Father Rubeo was delighted with the life and structure Saint Teresa had established for the Sisters at Saint Joseph's, and he was "moved to tears."[83] He gave her permission to set up more foundations, "as many as the hairs on her head."[84] In Teresa's first foundation, Father Rubeo saw the spirit of the Council of Trent, and he recognized that it was the answer to the decrees of the Church.[85]

No wonder Father Rubeo was impressed. He could hardly believe what she had accomplished "at a time when the [Carmelite] Order in Spain [was] in noticeable decline."[86] In God's providence and within a matter of months, the Superior General and Saint Teresa developed a relationship of mutual respect and admiration. Essentially, it became clear to both of them that they each needed the other in order to accomplish their mutual goals. Teresa needed permission to set up additional foundations, and the Carmelite General needed someone to spearhead the reform of the Carmelites in Spain. To his surprise, she requested permission to extend the reform to men, a request unheard of from a woman. Father Rubeo naturally balked at such an outlandish request. He was aware of how futile an effort this might be, because he himself had tried but failed to inspire any sort of change within the male branch of the Carmelites. How could a cloistered nun in a patriarchal society reform an order of men?

Despite his hesitation, he finally relented, giving her authorization to found two discalced monasteries for men. Saint Teresa was overjoyed, for she understood that unless both men and women in the Carmelite Order were willing to return to their fundamental roots, it would be impossible for her to succeed. She also recognized that the leadership of the monks would help to move things forward in the traditional Spanish culture of the time. For her, this was the fulfillment of a lifelong dream, yet it was quite a daunting task. The Superior General gave her the permission she needed to continue her work of reform, but in reality, he gave her little else. Here she was, a poor discalced nun, "loaded with patents and good wishes but devoid of all possibility of making them effective."[87]

At first glance, it might look as if Teresa did not have what it would take to accomplish this great work. Indeed, she did not have the financial or political means to make these changes become reality, but she was overflowing with both courage and hope, so in everything she saw a possibility. Saint Teresa was determined to create new foundations, so that through prayer, fewer souls would be lost. And, when it came to reforming the communities of men,

Teresa was not alone. Thankfully, John of the Cross was willing to help. John was a newly ordained Carmelite priest when he met Teresa, and even though he was half her age, he too longed for a more contemplative life. Teresa convinced him that he could find what he wanted, if only he would help her launch the kind of life she had in mind for the friars, a life that combined contemplation with an active apostolate.

With every new foundation, Teresa faced enormous challenges. She found herself entangled in lawsuits, mired in disputes over dowries, tied up in interminable bureaucratic red tape, included in the political infighting of the Church, and forced to deal with unscrupulous businessmen. The most serious trials came from the friars, who opposed any type of reform. Yet, over the course of twenty years, Saint Teresa founded and directed seventeen new monasteries of nuns who followed her vision of the Carmelite life, in addition to fifteen new monasteries for the friars.[88] An old Irish Jesuit, Father Hugh Kelly, wrote in 1945, describing the life of Teresa of Jesus during the years of the reform:

> Between the years of 1567 and 1582, a certain rather curious caravan must have been seen at one time or other on most of the roads of Spain. At the head of the caravan were a few friars in the brown white habit of the Carmelites, on foot or on mules; then came lumbering along a great wagon or cart on solid wooden wheels with no springs, closed in by a sack-cloth awning, and drawn by mules, with the muleteer walking at the side shouting at his animals.
>
> The close-drawn curtains gave no glimpse into the interior of the cart, and probably little view of the outer world to those within. Now and then, the animated voices of women might be heard; at intervals a small bell would tinkle and then would come the measured respon-

sive voices of women saying the office in choir.

There was constant inconvenience, and at times danger, as the great unwieldy thing crossed rickety bridges, got bogged down in morasses, or came in the way of a troop of bulls being driven to the bull fights. In summer, in a country "where the sun burns the hand holding the reins" it must have been intolerable within the awning — it was like going into Purgatory, the chief traveler used to say; in winter the cutting wind found entry through every chink.

At night, the caravan would stop at some miserable inn, where with luck a room might be got which could be isolated by curtains and would give some seclusion, though prayers and sleep would not be easy with the shouts of muleteers, gypsies, soldiers, or tramps. It was not a way of life conducive to spiritual contemplation or to authorship, or to the planning of a far-reaching movement of religious reform; yet it was the way of life of one of the great contemplatives, reformers, and writers in the years of her greatness. Everyone knew that in that caravan travelled Mother Teresa of Ávila in her work of reforming and founding.[89]

Old age set in for Saint Teresa when, in 1577, she fell down a flight of stairs at Saint Joseph's in Ávila and broke her left arm. Because it never completely healed, she was unable to dress herself or put on her own veil from that moment on. Thus, for the last five years of her life, her devoted companion and nurse, Sister Anna of Saint Bartholomew, accompanied her on her travels and cared for her. Even in this condition, however, Teresa continued her strenuous work, traveling to her convents and starting new communities. She also wrote *The Book of Her Foundations* and *The Interior Castle* during this time. However, this brutal schedule finally took its toll, and on September 29, 1582, in the city of Alba, an exhausted Teresa took to her bed, never to rise again. Her earthly travels had come to an end. No doubt it had all been a demanding journey, but it was a journey filled with hope, right up until the end.

It has been said that before death, scenes of your life pass before your inner eye. If this is true, what did Teresa see? The child sitting at her mother's knee reading tales of chivalry? Running away with her brother, both longing for martyrdom? The young and beautiful and flirtatious teenager? The joy of her profession at the Incarnation? The never-ending illnesses? The final conversion? The days at Saint Joseph's? The books? All of the journeys, the friendships, the joys and disappointments of a full life?

To be sure, Teresa knew that death was near, and she was prepared to welcome it. On the third of October, her failing strength could no longer be conquered by her will, and after receiving Holy Communion, she clasped her hands and cried out: "Oh my Lord and my Spouse, at last the longed-for hour has come; at last we shall see each other! I am a daughter of the Church."[90]

As the story goes, Sister Anna remained at Saint Teresa's side until the end, holding her hand and embracing her head until her breathing ceased on the evening of October 4, 1582.

Saint Teresa of Ávila, pray for us!

Reflection Questions

What are the highlights of the life and teachings of Saint Teresa of Ávila? How would you explain them to another person?

How can Teresa's motto, "Do what you are doing," help us in our daily lives?

Teresa was deeply rooted in the Christian virtue of hope. Think of an example from her life when this was especially true.

Part Two
Saint Catherine of Siena

In the light of faith I hope; suffer
me not to faint by the way.

WOMAN OF WISDOM

Saint Catherine of Siena lived during a time of upheaval, change, insecurity, and fear of the future.[1] It was also a time of war, natural calamities, persecution, and confusion. The fourteenth century, "which saw the beginnings of the Renaissance, was a time in which much of the security of the Middle Ages was coming to an end, both in state and Church."[2] During this period, scores of people in the Church lost their faith due to corruption, decadence, and infidelity, particularly among certain members of the clergy. And yet, in her mere thirty-three years on earth, Saint Catherine ascended to the heights of holiness, leaving a legacy that is a treasure to the Church. Still today, she captivates us, precedes us in faith, and beckons us to follow.

While we may be tempted to think of ourselves as more sophisticated than our fourteenth-century ancestors, it is hard to deny that many of their concerns and anxieties are also our own.[3] Like Catherine, we live in challenging times, perhaps to a degree unknown in the past. We, too, are living in a time of upheaval. In our own day, there are wars and hostilities, poverty, violence, immorality, political corruption, and greed. And just as in Catherine's day, the faithful witnessed deep scandals in the Church, so in our own day the Church is undergoing real trials and difficulties.

Even though Catherine had no formal education, she spoke in a way that was relevant and helpful to her contemporaries. Therefore, we can trust that she can also speak to us. By approaching this wise woman from Siena with faith and confidence, we will find that she has solutions to a lot of the questions we face today.

When he declared Catherine Benincasa of Siena a saint on June 19, 1461, Pope Pius II referred to the young woman's "wisdom," which was not wisdom that she acquired over time and with great effort, but was rather an infused gift of the Holy Spirit. He claimed that "no one approached her without leaving her with their minds and hearts more informed and better. Her knowledge came down to her from heaven; henceforth she could teach without having had masters."[4] And five hundred years later, when Pope Saint Paul VI named her a Doctor of the Church on October 4, 1970, he again mentioned Catherine's wisdom, saying: "What strikes us most about the Saint is her infused wisdom. That is to say, lucid, profound and inebriating absorption of the divine truths and the mysteries of the faith."[5]

More than anything, however, it was the power and warmth of her words that drew people to Catherine. Blessed Raymond of Capua,[6] Catherine's confessor, biographer, and intimate friend, wrote that Catherine could talk about the things of God "for a hundred days and nights without stopping for any food or drink. She never tired of talking about God; on the contrary, as time went on, she seemed to grow ever more enthusiastic."[7] Those in her presence experienced such a joy and vitality that you can almost hear them saying to each other, "It is well that we are here" (Mt 17:4).

Four years after her death, Father Raymond wrote his own book on Catherine, entitled *The Life of Saint Catherine of Siena*, in which he describes events from her life that only someone very close to her could know. Today, much of what is known about Catherine is thanks to Father Raymond of Capua and his book.

FAMILY LIFE

Catherine's story begins in the central part of Italy, just south of Florence. Nestled in the countryside, surrounded by gently sloping vineyards, is the small city of Siena. In Catherine's time,

Siena was an important medieval city, complete with the impressive University of Siena. In true Italian style, life centered around the village square, the Piazza del Campo, as well as the Duomo, Siena's magnificent cathedral. Throughout the city, quaint, shuttered houses with curved doorways lined the narrow, winding streets.

Catherine was born in this village on the Feast of the Annunciation, March 25, 1347. From an historical perspective, some might think it unfortunate that Catherine came into the world in the middle of the fourteenth century, just missing by a few decades the thirteenth, which some believe was the greatest of centuries. The thirteenth century was a witness to the majesty of the Catholic Church. Those days of glory included the building of Gothic cathedrals and the flowering of religious orders. This was the time of great saints such as Dominic, Francis, Bonaventure, Albert the Great, Thomas Aquinas, and so many others. It was also a time of learning and achievement, with the founding of universities and the beginning of representative governments in parts of Europe.

In God's plan, however, Catherine's entrance into the world followed these religious luminaries and cultural achievements. At the time of her birth, the great religious orders were in decline. The Hundred Years' War[8] was raging between France and England, and the Black Plague[9] was decimating the population of Western Europe. As a matter of fact, in the very year that Catherine was born, more than one hundred of the nearly 300 friars in the Dominican community of Santa Maria Novella in Florence died from the plague, and very few young men entered the order. And so, rather than being born into the greatest of centuries, Catherine was born into one that was downright miserable!

The introductory pages of *The Decameron,* a book by the famous Italian author and poet Giovanni Boccaccio, portray something of the uncertainty, superstition, and desolation that enveloped Europe during the close of the Middle Ages. In woeful prose, Boccaccio describes the plague: "[It] struck such fear into the hearts of men and women that brother abandoned brother, uncle abandoned nephew, sister left brother, and very often wife abandoned husband, and even worse, almost unbelievable — fathers and mothers neglected to tend and care for their children as if they were not their own."[10]

In spite of this ongoing turmoil, Catherine's large family welcomed her arrival, along with her twin sister, Giovanna, who died shortly after birth. Catherine, blessedly healthy, was the second to the last of twenty-five children born to Lapa and Giacomo Benincasa. From the beginning, Catherine was set apart, in that she was the only child in the family that her mother was able to nurse. Giacomo, who went by the nickname Jacopo, ran the family's wool dying business. He was a mild-mannered man of faith, uprightness, and virtue. Catherine's mother played the more traditional role of the "Italian mama." She directed all the affairs in the home, and it was the job of Jacopo and the children to obey.

Soon after her birth, Catherine's older siblings began to marry, and the next generation of Benincasas quickly followed. Catherine's family home was rarely quiet, and relatives of all ages frequently visited. It was a home bustling with the activity of a large Italian family, complete with the joy of laughter and the lively disagreements that inevitably occurred around the dinner table. This full family life nurtured Catherine in her young, formative years.

Catherine's Vision

Providentially, Catherine lived near the Basilica of San Domenico, so she had regular access to the sacraments and the preaching of the Dominican fathers. No doubt her frequent contact with the Dominican priests and sisters accounted for the depth of her knowledge of Sacred Scripture, particularly Saint Paul's writings, and the teachings of another great Dominican, Saint Thomas Aquinas. Within this rich environment, Catherine experienced the grace of the Holy Spirit in a special way. It is not surprising, then, that one so deeply in love with God, and so profoundly aware of spiritual realities, was also full of joy. In fact, within the family, her pet name was Euphrosyne, after a Greek saint whose name means "joy-filled."

Saint Catherine was just a child when she began to think about God nearly all the time. Unlike her friends and companions, she started to embark on a spiritual journey that few could understand. This dramatic journey began when six-year-old Catherine had her first vision while she was returning home from a walk with her older brother, Stefano. In his book, *The Life of Saint Catherine of Siena*, Father Raymond of Capua describes this remarkable event:

> Hanging in the air in front of her over the roof of the [Dominican] church, she saw a most beautiful bridal chamber decked out in regal splendor, in which, on an imperial throne, dressed in pontifical attire and with a papal tiara on His head, sat the Lord Jesus Christ, the Savior of the world. With him were the Princes of the Apostles Peter and Paul and the holy Evangelist John. At the sight of all this the little girl remained rooted to the ground, gazing lovingly with unblinking eyes upon her Lord and Savior, who was revealing Himself to her in this way in order to captivate her love. Then, gazing straight at her with eyes full of majesty, and smiling most lovingly, He raised His right hand over her, made the sign of the cross of salvation like a priest, and graciously gave her His eternal benediction.[11]

As we can well imagine, the blessing from this extraordinary experience affected Catherine for the rest of her life. All at once, it became both a prophetic image of her future mission, and a betrothal to her beloved spouse. For an instant, Catherine had experienced the fire of divine love, a love that surpassed any earthly attachment. After that, "it became clear from Catherine's virtues, the gravity of her behavior, and her extraordinary wisdom, that under her girlish appearance, there was hidden a fully formed woman."[12] Forevermore, she would refer to the pope as her "sweet Christ on earth." Catherine went on to live the life of a mystic. She was privileged in that she had direct communication with God and insight into mysteries that transcend ordinary human knowledge. In other words, even at this young age, she enjoyed complete union with God.

With the Holy Spirit as her teacher, and without the aid of books, Catherine learned about the lives of holy men and women who dedicated themselves to Jesus Christ in a total and uncompromising way. They captivated her imagination, and she was eager to follow their example. With this in mind, little Catherine set off one day to become a hermit. She equipped herself for this new life with only a loaf of bread under her arm, and passing through the city gates, she eventually found a cave in which to pray. It was a long day for such a little girl, and by evening she was back at the family table without anyone noticing her absence. With time, this childish escapade faded from her memory, but her desire for holiness remained. Wishing for time alone with God, Catherine sought solitude in her own home and also in the Basilica of San Domenico. Her father eventually allowed her to create her own cell in a simple room downstairs. There she could be alone during her times of prayer and her acts of penance, which increased as time went on.

Catherine's fascination with those who withdrew from the attachments of the world in order to direct their attention to

God prompted her to embrace this kind of ascetic life. On her own, she began to choose the discomforts of harsh living conditions over those that provided pleasure and comfort. Even as a young child she made the resolution to use a rock as her pillow. These ideas and practices certainly separated her from the other small children in the town, and yet, she was the darling of her family and her community. She affected all who spent time with her, lifting their spirits and turning their hearts toward God. Because she was an inspiration to a number of young girls, they frequently gathered around her, eager to hear her speak about Jesus and his salvation.

Conflict at Home

Eventually Catherine's pursuit of holiness began to cause conflict at home. Unbeknownst to her family, after she saw the vision of Christ, young Catherine made a secret vow of virginity, and she had no intention of deviating from this. Still, as she approached marriageable age, her mother began searching for a suitable husband. Before long, this great saint and her mother were at odds with one another. To give us some insight into Catherine's personality, Father Raymond recounts the story of what happened next:

> The holy maiden kept on making [her refusal to marry]
> quite clear in every way, but her parents decided to force
> her and went to see one of the Order of Preaching Friars, a friend of the family, who is still alive.
>
> They implored him to try to persuade her to give
> way and this he promised to do; and in fact he went to
> see the virgin, and finding her firm in her holy intention, felt bound in conscience to give her this sensible
> advice: "Since there seems to be absolutely no doubt that
> you wish to serve the Lord," he said, "and these people
> keep pestering you to do the opposite, show them you

mean what you say — cut your hair off, and then perhaps they'll keep quiet!"

Accepting this advice as though it came from heaven, Catherine seized a pair of scissors and joyfully cut her hair off to the roots. ... Then she covered her head with a cap. From then on ... she began to go about in a veiled cap.

When her mother Lapa noticed this she asked her why she was wearing this strange kind of headgear, but she could not get any precise answer out of her, for Catherine did not want to lie ... and so she mumbled instead of replying openly; whereupon her mother went up to her, snatched the cap off her head, and found her head close-cropped.

This gave her a big shock, for Catherine had had very beautiful hair. "Whatever have you done daughter?" she wailed. Catherine simply put the cap back on her head and walked away, but Lapa's shrieks had brought her husband and sons running up, and when they discovered what had happened, they were furious with the girl.[13]

Friction with various other family members ensued, and because of her actions, Catherine received the punishment of serving as the family maid: cleaning, cooking, serving at table, and sharing her younger brother's room. These punishments might seem harsh, but they taught Catherine the virtues of obedience and self-denial. While she did all of this with joy, she remained constant in her determination to follow God's will for her life.

Sisters of Penance of Saint Dominic

In spite of all the protestations from different family members, Catherine was adamant that she must obey God, rather than man. Her father was eventually given the grace to recognize that his daughter was set apart for God in a very special way. This realization may have been the result of a vision he had when he entered the room while his daughter was on her knees praying. At that very moment, a white dove hovered above Catherine's head. It flew away as soon as he entered. When he questioned her, she knew nothing about it.[14] Believing that this was a sign from the Holy Spirit, her father prohibited any further interference with Catherine's decision not to marry, so that she could be faithful to her vow of virginity.

After this encounter, Catherine received permission to retreat to her own room, a holy sanctuary where she could return to her practices of prayer and penance. Even though her time alone was infrequent, she built for herself a "cell not made with human hands."[15] Here "she found the desert within her own house and solitude in the midst of people."[16] Because of this, Catherine was able to maintain her peace by imagining her father as our Lord and Savior Jesus Christ, her mother as his most glorious Mother, and the other members of her family as the holy apostles and disciples.[17] These images gave her the desire to serve her family joyfully, and with great patience.

Around this time, Catherine had a dream in which a number of the holy Fathers of the early Church and the founders of religious orders appeared to her. In her dream, each of the holy men and women advised her to follow his or her path to holiness, but Catherine's eyes remained fixed on the figure of Saint Dominic. As Catherine moved slowly toward him, Dominic came forward, holding out to her the habit of the Sisters of Penance of Saint Dominic. This great saint spoke to the young girl, saying: "Sweetest daughter, take courage and fear no obstacle, for you will undoubtedly put on this habit, as is your wish."[18]

Catherine was familiar with the Sisters of Penance of Saint Dominic and the work they did in Siena. These women were called the Mantellate because of the mantle, or cape, they wore over their habit whenever they were out in the city. When she was sixteen years old, Catherine asked her parents for permission to join the order, and not surprisingly, they opposed this idea. But Catherine prevailed, and her mother reluctantly agreed to visit the sisters to ask permission for her daughter to enter.

The Sisters of Penance, a fraternity of Saint Dominic, was a community of widows who lived in their own homes rather than in a convent. Normally, the women who joined their ranks were mature, with most of the demands of marriage and family behind them. They worked in the streets of the city caring for the poor and needy, which included both men and women. In doing such work, they had to avoid any sign of scandal. As a result, the sisters refused the request of Catherine's mother, believing that it was improper for a girl of marriageable age to take up their work.

Once again, Catherine's determination, coupled with a mysterious illness, resulted in her getting her way. Here, Father Raymond fills in the details of this encounter:

> Poor Lapa remained at her bedside, applying what remedies she could and doing her best to cheer up her daughter. Even though Catherine was weak in body she was stronger than ever in intention, and seeing that this might be a good moment to get her mother to do what she wanted, she said rather slyly, "Mother, if you want me to be well and strong again, satisfy my one wish, which is to receive the habit of the Sisters of Penance of Saint Dominic. If you don't, I'm afraid that both God and Saint Dominic will see to it that you don't have me with you in any kind of habit."[19]

It is interesting to note that the main concern of the Sisters of

Penance was the potential scandal of having an attractive girl in their ranks. And yet it is no coincidence that of all the female saints, Catherine is one of the few who was not necessarily physically beautiful or even pretty. The ugly blisters and sores from her illness accentuated this fact. Ironically, Catherine's mysterious illness was what led the sisters to accept her into their community. Within a few days of this decision, Catherine's ailment disappeared, and she received the Dominican habit just as Saint Dominic had promised her.

Reflection Questions

The Black Plague struck such fear in the hearts of men and women that families were willing to abandon one another. We witnessed a similar reaction of fear (though thankfully not usually so stark) during the COVID-19 pandemic. From what we know, is this rational? How do you make sense of the fear people feel in the face of such suffering?

In naming Catherine a Doctor of the Church, Pope Paul VI spoke about her infused wisdom. What exactly is wisdom, and how do you know if someone has it?

"I AM HE WHO IS"

A new season of Catherine's life began when she entered the Sisters of Penance. At the tender age of sixteen, she was young by today's standards, but in fourteenth-century Siena, Catherine was an adult and was treated as such. As a member of the Mantellate, and responding to the rules of their community, Catherine continued to live in her family home. In this familiar setting, she spent her time in prayer, leaving only to attend Mass or to go to confession.

For three continuous years, which served as a kind of private novitiate, God blessed Catherine with numerous visions. He came to her often as a friend and teacher. In fact, he "appeared to her spiritual eyes [and] instructed her in the secret mysteries of the Divinity."[20] During these mystical experiences and spiritual revelations, Catherine's room was often filled with the fragrance of lilies, and the saints were heard singing songs of praise.

Throughout this time of prolonged retreat, even though she was in her own home and was surrounded by others, Catherine lived a life of silence and solitude. Christ was her only companion, and the two of them conversed and spent time together in prayer. Other than these divine conversations, Catherine spoke only to her confessor. This is Father Raymond's explanation of this time in Catherine's life:

> To observe the vow of purity better, Catherine decided to preserve an utter silence and never speak except at confession. My predecessor as her confessor has written that for three years, she never spoke a word to anyone except him, and then only when she was making her confession. ...
>
> She lived continually enclosed in her little cell, only emerging from it to go to church. She had no need to leave it for meals, for all she needed to eat she could eat there — her only cooked food was bread.[21]

At the very beginning of these visions and revelations, the Lord delivered to her the simple doctrine that became the basis of her whole understanding of God and humanity:

> Do you know, daughter, who you are, and who I am? If you know these two things, you will be blessed. You are she who is not; whereas I am He who is. Have this

knowledge in your soul and the Enemy will never de-
ceive you and you will escape all his wiles; you will never
disobey my commandments and will acquire all grace,
truth, and light.[22]

With this message, Catherine was given a profound insight into
the reality of God and the reality of man. She understood that
when God said, "I am He who is,"[23] he was expressing the truth
about his very nature as Creator, in that he is the origin of everything that exists. This was why Saint Catherine always referred
to God as First Truth. Understanding this is key to everything
she teaches. Truth for her always relates to being — to the wonder of reality itself, a beauty that comes from and goes to love,
divine love. Knowing this helped Catherine, and it can help all
of us to understand our place in the universe. It also helps us to
order our lives toward God. In other words, we can truly see that
he "is," and we and all of creation "are not."

This knowledge became even more important as Catherine
recognized how deeply sin affects our relationship with God,
and is therefore responsible for the gulf that separates us from
him. In fact, this is the basis for Catherine's teaching on the
Christ-Bridge, in which she claims that Christ is the bridge we
must cross if we want to get from earth to heaven. This deep
understanding of who God is and who we are formed the bed-
rock of Catherine's theology, and it had a dramatic impact on her
spiritual life. She referred to this reality as "the cell of self-knowledge." In her book entitled *Passion for the Truth: Compassion for
Humanity*, Sister Mary O'Driscoll, OP, explains how Catherine
understood the meaning of self-knowledge:

Self-knowledge, in the sense in which Catherine uses
the term, is not a morbid introspection, nor is it merely
a psychological self-understanding. It is rather a knowl-

edge of self which we gain by looking at ourselves in the light of the One who created us.

This does not mean that Catherine is not concerned with true self-knowledge, but rather that she realizes that although we can come so far in understanding ourselves by looking at ourselves, we can never arrive at the deepest, richest self-understanding without seeing ourselves through God's eyes, or as she puts it, without gazing at ourselves in the "gentle mirror" of God. ...

Self-knowledge is really a double knowledge: It is a knowledge of ourselves acquired by looking at God, and a knowledge of God acquired by reflecting on God's goodness toward us. ...

Through self-knowledge, we come to appreciate both our dignity and our "nothingness."[24]

Love of God and Love of Neighbor

Sometime before Catherine's twentieth birthday, to her great disappointment, she learned that her time of solitude had come to an end. Apparently, without warning, Jesus gently told Catherine: "Go, it is dinner time, and the rest of the family are about to sit down at table; go and be with them, and then come back to me."[25] Catherine reacted by asking the Lord whether she had done something to offend him. She was afraid that if she mingled once again with other people, she might lose some of her contemplative spirit.[26] Jesus lovingly chastised her, reminding her of the double precept of love: to love God *and* to love one's neighbor. "You must walk, in fact, with both feet, not one, and with two wings fly to heaven!"[27] In prayer, she confessed to God her fears, and she received this most beautiful reply:

I have no intention whatever of parting you from myself, but rather of making sure you bind to me all the closer by the bond of your love for your neighbor. Remember that I have laid down two commandments of love: love of me and love of your neighbor. ... It is the justice of these two commandments that I want you now to fulfill. *On two feet you must walk my way.*[28]

From then on, twenty-one-year-old Catherine "walked firmly on the two feet of love of God and love of neighbor, of prayer and action."[29] She began to demonstrate her love for God by loving others. Recognizing the importance of this and living it out may be one of Saint Catherine's greatest contributions to Christian spirituality. Essentially, she lived her life based on the truth that the love of God and the love of neighbor are inseparable, and that they increase or decrease proportionately. This was a pivotal event in Catherine's life. The grace she received in the private, loving embrace of the Father, she now dedicated to the salvation of souls. Soon this became her most important work and the greatest desire of her heart.

That being said, it wasn't easy for Catherine to leave the privacy of her cell. She reentered the world slowly, initially by moving out into the circle of her family. It is often true that when God calls us to love our neighbors, he intends for us to start with those closest to us. It was no different for Catherine, and so she intentionally humbled herself, and tried to love each family member without reserve. As before, she spent her time helping with the cooking and cleaning, but now, rather than it being a punishment, Catherine used it to bring Christ's love to all, and to see him in everyone she encountered.

Soon her world expanded into the streets of Siena, where she nursed the sick and gave food and alms to the poor. In fact, those in need frequently came to the door of the Benincasa home, because they knew that Catherine would give them something. And she did not disappoint. She gave them food, clothing, and anything else in the house that could be spared — and even some things that couldn't!

Call to Action

From a worldly point of view, Catherine of Siena was nothing more than a humble servant of God, spending most of her time in service to the poor. When she began her public ministry, the tenor of life in Siena was as turbulent as it was throughout the rest of fourteenth-century Europe. War was the perpetual backdrop — war between England and France, war between the Italian city-states, war between neighborhoods, and even war between families. In Siena, families were notorious for their frequent conflicts, and they passed their family feuds from one generation to another in much the same way as family heirlooms. In fact, it took the finality of the plague, which swept across the country at regular intervals, to settle these old scores.

It was into this violent world that God asked Catherine to carry his message of love and mercy. She was fearless in her approach, as Christ had planted within her a zeal for souls. When she was still young, he said to her: "Open to me, my sister, my beloved, my dove. ... Open for me the gates of souls that I may enter them. Open the path by which my sheep may pass in and out and find pasture. Open for me your treasury of grace and knowledge and pour it out upon the faithful."[30]

Indeed, wherever she went, Catherine did open the gates of souls who were desperately in need of God's love and mercy. In her book, *The Way of the Mystics*, Hilda Graef spoke in glowing terms about the physical and spiritual healing that Catherine brought to the overall chaos of the day:

> It is one of the most consoling facts that mystics seem to flourish especially in turbulent times. The graces of contemplative prayer need but a pure heart in which to

take root, however much the world may be torn by wars and unrest. There is no more striking example of the mystic life lived in the turmoil of the world than that of St. Catherine of Siena.[31]

An extreme example of this healing came when Catherine was assigned to care for another member of the Mantellate named Andrea, who had been abandoned by her family and was dying of breast cancer. Catherine's cheerful demeanor grated on her embittered patient, so much so that Andrea began to spread rumors, telling people that she doubted that Catherine was living a chaste life. Catherine insisted that she was still a virgin, but it was too late; the rumor had already spread to the other Mantellate. It had even reached her mother, and Lapa railed at Catherine for taking care of such a vile woman. Eventually, however, Andrea softened and accepted Catherine's help. For Catherine, cleaning the wound on Andrea's breast was nauseating. In principle, she dearly wanted to embrace suffering in whatever form it appeared, but this was disgusting. To overcome her repulsion, Catherine literally sucked the pus from the wound out of her love for God and love for her neighbor. Years later, she told Raymond that she had never tasted anything so sweet.

Despite her busy schedule working the streets of Siena from morning until night, Catherine was still able to balance both contemplation and action. For Catherine, action and contemplation were not alternatives or opposites. Instead, she saw that they complement one another, since neither is complete without the other. This teaching is all the more relevant in today's society, where we live in a continuous race against time. Catherine teaches us that prayer is more than just a refueling activity in order to resume our busy lives. It is more than simply a holy rest from work. Rather, everything that she experienced in contemplation propelled her to action and every action was present and part of her prayer.[32]

Because of this inner power, fueled by her hope and trust in the Lord, Catherine was a woman of influence, and her witness and teaching became the impetus for countless conversions. Talk of her holiness spread, and people from all over Italy, including the pope, began to seek her advice and to ask for prayers for family members who were ill or committing grave sin. Others wrote letters that required a response. For the most part, Catherine could neither read nor write.[33] So it was necessary for her to dictate her correspondence to one or more of her followers. Using this method, Catherine became one of the greatest letter-writers of her century. In fact, one of the best ways to appreciate Saint Catherine's personality, not to mention her theology and spirituality, is through a careful reading of her letters. In his biography of Saint Catherine, Edmund Gardner describes the recipients of these letters:

> They are written to men and women in every walk of life and every level of society. Her varied correspondents include a mendicant in Florence, a Jewish banker in Padua, two sovereign pontiffs and three kings.
>
> Leaders of armies, rulers of Italian republics, receive her burning words and bow to her inspired will, just as often as do private citizens seeking her counsel in the spiritual life, or simple monks and hermits in their cells striving to find the way of perfection.
>
> She was able to warn a queen ... while she bids the wife of a tailor, "Clothe yourself in the royal virtues." Her wonderful, all-embracing and intuitive sympathy knows no barriers, but penetrates into the house of shame as well as into the monastery.[34]

Catherine's Followers

Catherine's followers were of various ages and states of life, and all were attracted to her charismatic personality and the way she lived her life. They served as her scribes and joined her in prayer and in her charitable activities. She considered these disciples her spiritual children and members of her spiritual family. A lot of them were older than she, yet they often referred to her as "Mama." Here, Father Raymond speaks to the dedication of her followers:

> Catherine was accompanied by a great number of men and women. There would have been many more too if she had not stopped them. Those who went with her put themselves in the hands of God's providence by voluntary poverty, preferring to go on pilgrimage with the virgin and beg for their food rather than stay at home where they lacked for nothing — except that they would have been deprived of her sweet and wholesome company.[35]

In Catherine's day, this way of living the religious life was new and somewhat controversial. Back then, it was a radical departure from the role of women in public affairs, and it was also in conflict with Catherine's own lifestyle, so her decision to travel outside of Siena had to be well considered. Her detractors failed to understand the need for her to travel to numerous places and with such a large group. Because of this criticism, Catherine asked the pope to send his requests for her help in writing for all to see. She addresses this in a letter to Father Raymond:

> Father, many of our citizens and their wives and also some of the nuns of my own order are quite scandalized by all the journeys — too many, they say — I have hitherto made to one place and another. [They] say that it is not right for a religious virgin to travel about so much [and with so many followers].

I myself am quite sure that I have not done anything wrong by undertaking these journeys, because wherever I have gone it has been in obedience to God and His Vicar and for the good of souls; still, to avoid giving further scandal, I propose for the moment to stay where I am.

But if the Vicar of Christ insists that I come, let his will be done and not mine. In this case, make sure that his will is set down in writing, so that the people who are inclined to be scandalized may see quite clearly that I am not going off just because I want to.[36]

Even in the midst of this controversy, Saint Catherine's reputation for holiness and good counsel continued to spread throughout Italy. By 1372, at the age of twenty-five, Catherine was helping to resolve disagreements among rival families not only in Siena, but also in Pisa and other Italian cities. In May of 1374, she traveled to Florence, and in that same year Pope Gregory XI requested her prayers for the unity of the Church and his leadership in that effort. Before long, she found herself as a participant in trying to resolve some of the most complex political problems.

This phase of Saint Catherine's active life is notable because during this time she wrote the majority of her letters, as well as her principal work, *The Dialogue*. By now, Catherine understood that being a peacemaker was her opportunity to follow in the footsteps of her beloved Jesus Christ — the greatest peacemaker — and the "bridge" between God and humanity.[37]

Reflection Questions
How does Catherine's understanding of self-knowledge differ from what we might find in a self-help book?

How do you balance action and contemplation? Catherine did it, but is this even possible in the busy world in which we live?

POLITICS, THE PAPACY, AND THE GREAT WESTERN SCHISM

In the fourteenth century of Saint Catherine of Siena, the Catholic Church dominated the external political world just as it regulated the personal and spiritual life of every individual. Every event of significance, religious or not, revolved around the Church. However, the world as Catherine knew it was in a state of constant flux. It was a time in which individual countries in western Europe had begun to develop a sense of national and ethnic identity, as well as their own economy. Each and every shift from Church to state confronted and disrupted the unity of medieval Christendom, which had always permitted the dominance of papal power in political as well as religious matters.[38] In light of this, Catherine's political and ecclesial activities were a large part of the final six years of her life, until her death at the age of thirty-three. Her motive in this is clear: the desire for unity in the Church.

In April 1376, news reached Catherine that the city of Florence was under papal interdict. The issue at hand pertained to a tax levy the city of Florence had imposed on its priests, which had an overall effect on the finances of the Church. Catherine left Siena in May and went to Florence, where she offered to mediate the situation between the city and the reigning pope, Gregory XI. The offer was accepted. Shortly after her trip to Florence, she moved on to France and arrived in Avignon, the home of Pope Gregory, on June 18, 1376. The fact that the pope, the Bishop of Rome, actually lived in Avignon, France, deserves an explanation.

The Avignon Papacy

More often than not, the events that shape a specific time period are the direct result of what came before. For example, the political and clerical situation in which Catherine found herself came about over many years and through much upheaval, unrest, and confusion. It started at the end of the thirteenth century, during the pontificate of Pope Boniface VIII (1294–1303). During his short reign, Boniface attempted to maintain the powers of the papacy, and the independence of the Church from secular influence. In doing so, he encountered great opposition from Philip IV, King of France. Philip had no qualms about opposing the head of the Church. In fact, he was ruthless. Boniface challenged Philip in 1302, issuing a papal document that he titled "One, Holy" (*Unam Sanctam*), which asserted that the pope had supreme authority in both religious and secular affairs and that "it [was] necessary that every human creature be subject to the Roman Pontiff."[39]

In retaliation, Philip sent his troops to arrest Boniface. They tortured the elderly pope, and he died shortly thereafter. To this day, the conflict between Pope Boniface and the King of France represents one of the more dramatic clashes between the forces of Church and state. After Boniface's death, the cardinals met for eleven months before they decided to elect a Frenchman, Clement V (1264–1314), as pope. Clement rejected the idea of going to Rome for his coronation, and he chose instead to begin his papacy in Lyons, France, in the presence of King Philip IV. Clement never returned the papacy to Rome, and in spite of the efforts of some of his successors, the papacy remained in Avignon for the next seventy years.[40]

During this era, abuses in the Church took several forms, but none were more serious than those which developed as a result of the Avignon Papacy. This move from Italy to France, which Clement V contrived, ushered in a sorrowful time in the life of the Church. Many associated the decadence of the papacy with its presence in Avignon. Listen to what Petrarch, the famous Italian poet, has to say:

Instead of holy solitude we find a criminal host and
crowds of the most infamous satellites; instead of sober-
ness, licentious banquets; instead of pious pilgrimages,
preternatural and foul sloth; instead of the bare feet of the
apostles, the snowy coursers of [bandits] fly past us, the
horses bedecked in gold and fed on gold, soon to be shod
with gold, if the Lord does not check this slavish luxury.
… O, ye unkempt and emaciated old men, is it for this
that you labored? Is it for this that you have sown the field
of the Lord and watered it with your holy blood?[41]

While this was a scathing indictment of the situation in Avignon,
to blame the Church's problems solely on the location in which
the pope resided would be to ignore a lot of the other factors that
caused concern. Even so, no one can deny that the Church was
suffering and was in desperate need of reform, all while the pope
was living Avignon. For Catherine,

Avignon symbolized the dissipation and corruption that
was eroding the soul of the Church. It stood for everything that she was struggling against. … It was said that
she had the preternatural ability to *smell* sin. She always
knew when one of her male followers had surrendered
to carnal desires — one sniff and she would send him
off to confession. … [To Catherine], Avignon was a sin-
ful place and she did not want to spend any more time
there than was absolutely necessary.[42]

Go Back to Rome

This brings us back to why Catherine, accompanied by Father
Raymond, was in Avignon in June of 1376. They had left Florence, where they had met with government officials, and then
journeyed to Avignon with three specific goals in mind. First,

they came to mediate and reach a solution to the disagreements between the city of Florence and the papacy. Second, due to the Muslim occupation of Jerusalem, Catherine came to urge the pope to call a crusade, which she and others believed would solve the problem of disunity in the Church, giving Christians a common enemy, so to speak. Finally, and most importantly, Catherine traveled to Avignon to beg Pope Gregory to return the papacy to its rightful home in Rome. Catherine had already corresponded with the pope about this. Four of her still-existing letters to Gregory were written prior to her arrival in Avignon; an additional six letters were written while she was there. Like it or not, Pope Gregory XI was soon to encounter the spiritual force and great wisdom of Catherine of Siena.[43]

Two days after she arrived in Avignon, Catherine had her first audience with Pope Gregory. When he appeared, he proved to be a man "short of stature, pale, with grave gestures and sorrowful eyes."[44] At first, he was rather aloof, as the boldness and familiarity of her letters had unsettled him. But as they spoke, he warmed up to her, and like others before him, he found her charismatic personality quite appealing. They began their relationship by discussing the peace pact between Florence and the papacy, which proved to be a futile effort for both Catherine and the pope. The Florentines had refused to compromise; the disagreements between Florence and the papacy were complex, and they reflected the political and religious undercurrents of this troubled time. Throughout the late Middle Ages, the Holy Roman Empire and the papacy engaged in periodic power struggles, and like most things in life, it was usually over money. The Florentines also resented the long absence of the popes from Rome and the excessive influence of the French.

Although the Florence reconciliation failed to materialize, Catherine still had a list of things to discuss with Pope Gregory. She stayed for three months, and they met several times, presumably to discuss what it would take to get Gregory back to Rome, where he belonged. As the months passed, her pleas became more and more urgent. They included arguments against his personal uncertainties, as well as the negative influence of his cardinals, who persistently fed him tales of danger and regret should he return to Rome. In his book, *Catherine of Siena: A Passionate Life*, author Don Brody illustrates the essence of these conversations: "They talked and talked. Gregory, whose natural tendency was vacillation, was emboldened by her confidence that his return to Rome was God's will. The more they talked, the more he believed it. But after she left his presence other courtiers would get his ear to suggest the move was unwise, or untimely, or dangerous, and Gregory became anxious again."[45]

After much back and forth and threats from all sides, eventually Catherine was successful in reaching her final goal. She finally persuaded the Holy Father to return to the See of Saint Peter by boldly reminding him of a secret vow that he had with God (which God revealed to Catherine), in which he had promised to move the papacy back to Rome. Because Catherine had no natural way of knowing about this vow, Pope Gregory considered this conversation to be a supernatural sign from God, and he subsequently agreed to leave Avignon for the Eternal City.

For Catherine, all the worry and stress seemed worth it when Gregory finally announced his intention to make the move from Avignon to Rome. To prepare for his arrival, his aides were sent ahead to Italy to let the Romans know he was coming. On September 13, Pope Gregory XI left his papal palace in Avignon for the last time, "stepping over the prostrate form of his father who had thrown himself on the ground in protest."[46] A few cardinals had opted to stay behind, but most joined the papal entourage despite their reservations about the dangers awaiting them in Rome. On October 2, 1376, they set sail for Italy.

Nothing speaks more eloquently of Catherine's influence than when the pope actually followed her instruction and departed for Italy. In September of 1376, Catherine left Avignon with the understanding that Pope Gregory would not be far behind. Always practical and wise, she realized that the opposing forces had not given up on Gregory, and that the pope would surely experience doubts and misgivings. So she remained in the city of Genoa until she received word that the papal entourage had positively begun to sail. To her great relief, Pope Gregory held fast to his promise, and on January 17, 1377, he solemnly entered the city of Rome. Catherine was undoubtedly God's messenger in this endeavor, not unlike the prophets of old, as she summoned Christ's Vicar on earth back to the truth of his vocation and calling. Saint Catherine was never to see Pope Gregory again.

After this momentous event, Catherine returned directly to Siena, and she turned her attention to establishing the monastery of Our Lady of the Angels. In doing this, she fulfilled her lifelong desire to build a convent for cloistered nuns, even though she herself remained a Third Order Dominican. Her respite in Siena did not last long, however, as Pope Gregory needed her skills once again. Not surprisingly, shortly after he settled in Rome, trouble broke out in Florence. The pope was quick to send Catherine to the Florentines as his mediator. Tragically, on March 27, 1378, only three short months after his triumphal return, Pope Gregory died suddenly. Without Gregory as her protector, Catherine fled Florence in the midst of deadly riots. Father Raymond speaks about this in his book:

> My good reader, I must tell you that when, in an endeavor to bring peace between the shepherd and his sheep, this holy virgin was sent by Pope Gregory XI of happy memory to the city of Florence, which had rebelled against the Church. She had to endure many unjust persecutions. These reached such a pitch that one Devil's

hireling rushed madly out upon her with a naked dag-
ger, and would certainly have killed her if the Lord had
not come to her rescue.[47]

Gregory's death marked the beginning of a new and final phase
of Catherine's public life. Her work for peace and unity was
hardly over. In fact, in many ways, it was just beginning.

Schism and the Antipopes

Shortly after Gregory's death, the cardinals met in Rome to select
a new pope. In what proved to be one of the more memorable
conclaves in the history of the Church, they elected the Archbishop of Bari (Bartolomeo Prignano) to the papacy. An Italian,
he took the name Pope Urban VI. By the time of his coronation
at Saint Peter's Basilica two weeks later, the curia in Avignon, the
Holy Roman Empire, and other Catholic rulers had all heard the
news. The entire Christian world was aware of the new pope.

The cardinals who participated in the conclave knew Urban
VI to be an upright and moral man, but his zeal for reform, not
to mention his harshness and rigidity, soon left them questioning their decision. In fact, there are still letters which indicate
that Catherine herself tried to soften him. Nevertheless, his severe and uncompromising manner led some of the cardinals to
regret their choice. These dissenting cardinals claimed that they
were victims of coercion, due to the insistence on the part of the
Romans to elect an Italian (out of fear that the French would
move the papacy back to Avignon).

Even though they had no authority to do so, these same cardinals gathered secretly to select a new pope, who in turn took
the name Clement VII. The fact that two men claimed the rights
and title of pope sent shock waves around the world. As predicted, the disobedient cardinals and the new pope *did* reestablish
residence back in Avignon. Clement VII was the first antipope

of the Western Schism. France favored antipope Clement over Pope Urban, while England supported Pope Urban. Other European countries divided their loyalties between the two men, which caused great confusion among the faithful.

And with that, the Great Western Schism began. It split the western Church in two, causing division in countries, towns, parishes, religious orders, and families alike.[48] This assault on the Mystical Body of Christ broke Catherine's heart. She knew that the election of Urban VI as pope was valid, because once the cardinals elected a pope, they had no power to depose him and elect another. Therefore, Clement VII had no real claim to the papacy.

Pope Urban was no fool. He knew that something had to be done because of the seriousness of this situation. He had known of Catherine's support for his predecessor, and so he began to correspond with her. He pleaded with her to support him as pope and to fight to save the entire Church. In November of 1378, he summoned Catherine to Rome. It was during this time that she wrote her most impassioned prayers and letters, pleading with God and with her fellow believers to bring an end to the schism. According to Father Raymond, this is what happened when Catherine met with Pope Urban VI:

> The Supreme Pontiff was clearly delighted to see Catherine again and he asked her to say a few words of encouragement to the cardinals, especially with regard to the schism, which had then just begun. The virgin urged them with many arguments, which she expressed most felicitously, to be strong in constancy. She showed that divine providence is always with us, above all when the Church has to suffer, and ended by telling them not to be afraid of the schism and to do the things of God and to fear no one.[49]

Regrettably, before the schism was over, three different men laid claim to the papacy. Yet at all times, there was only one true pope. The other two were antipopes, each with his own following, his own cardinals, and his own administrative offices. The schism began in 1378 and did not end until 1417.

Reflection Questions

Today we are facing many Church/state issues, where the state is impinging on the rights of the Church. How is this playing out in the public square?

In our day and age, in which we can use technology for nearly everything, would it matter if the pope lived outside of Rome? Why or why not?

CATHERINE'S WRITINGS

Even though Catherine did not write great theological tomes or numerous volumes of texts, her teaching continues to enrich the doctrine of the Church. This saint from Siena teaches us about imitating Christ, his life, and his passion. In fact, all of her writings fall into three categories: her letters, her book entitled *The Dialogue of Divine Providence*, and her prayers.

Letters

We can glean much about Saint Catherine's involvement with the concerns of the Church from her carefully written letters. With each detail, these lengthy exhortations give us a window into the mystical experiences and spiritual insights that Catherine shared with cardinals, kings, and popes. Clearly, it is almost unthinkable that this uneducated woman, from a remote town in Italy, would be able to share such wisdom and have such influence over the affairs of men.

Catherine's supernatural wisdom was most certainly a gift from God, and she knew that apart from him, she was nothing and could do nothing. Catherine depended solely upon God's instructions, which she received in her intimate conversations with him. Consequently, both the content of Catherine's letters and her instructions for the leadership of the Church came from her times of deep prayer and from her conversations with the Creator. Her letters cover a period of about ten years (1370–80). Catherine wrote them to people of every station in life, from popes, kings and queens, to humble artisans and members of her own family. A total of 381 of her letters still exist.

We might wonder why a pope would listen to such a young woman, lacking a proper education and hailing from a small town in Italy. More importantly, why would such a woman believe that she could influence the pope? First of all, Catherine had a deep, abiding hope and complete faith in the Lord. Second, the answers to these questions are evident in Catherine's letters to both Pope Gregory XI and Pope Urban VI. Fourteen letters to Gregory and nine to Urban still exist, with the earliest dating from 1376. Whether Catherine wrote to the pope, to a friend, or to her mother, the style was the same. The opening paragraph always radiated a humble respect. She invokes the names of Jesus and Mary and continues by describing how undeserving she is to be writing such a letter.

Here is just one example of the beginning of a letter Catherine wrote to Pope Gregory XI urging him to return the papacy to Rome, using the metaphor of a fruitful tree:

In the name of Jesus Christ crucified and of sweet Mary:

To you, most reverend and beloved father in Christ Jesus, your unworthy, poor miserable daughter Catherine, servant and slave of the servants of Jesus Christ, writes in His precious Blood; with desire to see you as a fruitful tree, full of sweet and mellow fruits, and planted in fruitful earth — for if it were out of the earth the tree would dry up and bear no fruit.[50]

While this humility never disappeared, the tone in Catherine's letters could change drastically, depending upon the situation or the person who was the recipient. This style is reminiscent of Saint Paul, who makes himself all things to all men. "Are they Hebrews? So am I. Are they Israelites? So am I. Are they descendants of Abraham? So am I" (2 Cor 11:22). Whether the receiver needed compassion or encouragement, counsel or correction, praise or sympathy, Catherine gave to each accordingly and in abundance.

For example, in her letters to Pope Gregory, Catherine assured him that she understood his desire to lead the Church in reform, but she also recognized the obstacles blocking his path. Consequently, she appealed to his courage and sense of responsibility as the Shepherd of Christ's Church. Here is her plea:

> Therefore I said to you, Reverend Father, that I desired to see you firm and stable in your good resolution (since on this will follow the pacification of your rebellious sons and the reform of The Holy Church) and also to see you fulfil the desire felt by the servants of God, to behold you raise the standard of the most holy Cross against the infidels.[51]

She then followed up with another letter, again begging for Church reform:

> Do uproot in the garden of Holy Church the malodorous flowers, full of impurity and avarice, swollen with pride: that is, the bad priests and rulers who poison and rot that

garden. Ah me, you our Governor, do use your power to
pluck out those flowers! ... Plant in this garden fragrant
flowers, priests and rulers who are true servants of Jesus
Christ, and care for nothing but the honour of God and
the salvation of souls, and our fathers of the poor.[52]

In spite of her pleas, Catherine was a realist, and she knew only
too well that many powerful people opposed the pope's return to
Rome, and perhaps even more were against the reform of the clergy. In her letters, she forcefully corrected Pope Gregory, but at the
same time she defended him against those who reviled him, and
attacked the Church:

We lack nothing save virtue, and hunger for the salvation
of souls. But there is a remedy for this, father: that we flee
the love ... for ourselves and every creature apart from
God. Let no more note be given to friends or parents or
one's temporal needs, but only to virtue and the exalta-
tion of things spiritual. For temporal things are failing
you from no other cause than from your neglect of the
spiritual. ...

And if up to this time, we have not stood very firm,
I wish and pray in truth that the moment of time which
remains be dealt with manfully, following Christ, whose
vicar you are, like a strong man. And fear not, father, for
anything that may result from those tempestuous winds
that are now beating against you, those decaying members which have rebelled against you. Fear not; for divine
aid is near.

Have a care for spiritual things alone, for good shepherds, good rulers, in your cities — since on account of
bad shepherds and rulers you have encountered rebel-
lion. ...

And delay no longer, for many difficulties have occurred through delay. …

Pardon me, father, that I have said so many words
to you. You know that through the abundance of heart
the mouth speaketh. I am certain that if you shall be the
kind of tree I wish to see you, nothing will hinder you.[53]

Unfortunately, we no longer have a written response from Gregory to any of Saint Catherine's letters. However, we can intuit much
from her subsequent letters and actions. As the months went by,
her entreaties took on a more and more urgent tone. These letters included arguments against his personal uncertainties, and
against the influence of the cardinals who surrounded him with
tales of danger and regret, should he return to Rome.

Another one of her letters is worthy of mention, in that it calls
to mind how Catherine pursued the suffering soul just as our Father pursues us. Catherine wrote this letter to Francesco Malavolti,
a volatile, hot-blooded aristocrat who lived in Siena. When they
first met, Francesco was living a reckless and irresponsible lifestyle, as if he was somehow immortal. Once he encountered Catherine, however, he totally changed the focus of his life. He became
both a friend and disciple of the young virgin. While his intentions
were good, he fell and soon returned to his addictive behavior. Full
of shame, Francesco disappeared and did everything he could to
avoid meeting Catherine face to face.

After years of gazing at Our Lord, Saint Catherine knew that
"love pursues us even though we try to avoid its pressures and its
demands."[54] For this reason, she never stopped asking about her
friend, and she continued to search for him. Eventually, she wrote
Francesco this quite unforgettable letter:

Dearest and more than dearest son in Christ Gentle Jesus,

I, Caterina, servant and slave of the servants of Jesus Christ, am writing to you in his precious blood. I long to find you once again, little lost sheep! I long for this very deeply! And I long to put you back into the fold with your companions. But it seems to me the devil has so stolen you away as to make it impossible to find you again. I, your poor mother, am going about looking for you, sending for you, because I would like to put you on the shoulders of my sorrow and my compassion for your soul.

Open the eyes of your understanding, dearest son! Raise them above the darkness! Acknowledge your sin, not with spiritual dejection but with self-knowledge and trust in God's goodness. Look how wretchedly you have spent the fortune of grace your heavenly Father gave you. Then do as the prodigal son did who had spent his fortune in evil living. When he realized how destitute he had become, he acknowledged his failure and ran back to ask his father for mercy. You do the same. For you are impoverished and destitute, and your soul is dying of hunger.[55]

Not surprisingly, Francisco immediately ran to Catherine, "though not, he tells us, without great fear and shame."[56] Her response was more than he could have ever hoped:

But she, like the kindest and sweetest mother, received me with a joyful countenance, giving the greatest comfort to my weakness. And not many days later, when I went to her again, and one of the virgin's women companions said to her, in a rather querulous manner that I had very little stability, she said with a smile: Don't worry, my sisters, because he cannot escape out of my hands no matter which way he chooses to take.[57]

The letters that Catherine wrote (with the help of her scribes) are extraordinary and full of hope. This apostolic activity was a gift, not only to the recipient of the letter, but also to the rest of us. They give us a glimpse of Catherine's deep, compassionate love for each person with whom she corresponded. She added her own personal touch to each letter, as she responded with sensitivity and common sense to the particular joys and sorrows of her recipients.

Through this charitable activity, Catherine found a way to join her radical love for God with her undying love for her neighbor, translating her mystical encounters into the stuff of everyday life. Most importantly however, she was able to communicate this love to others because of the love she personally received in her own prayerful relationship with God. Essentially, each letter was part of her prayer.

The Dialogue of Divine Providence

Catherine wrote one book, entitled *The Dialogue of Divine Providence*, better known as *The Dialogue*. It is an exchange of questions and answers between Catherine and God the Father about the most important problems of humankind. These include discussions on the way of spiritual perfection, obedience, prayer, and Divine Providence, as well as other matters of importance to the Church and the society of her time. Although *The Dialogue* is not a clearly organized or systematic work, it does represent something of a synthesis of Saint Catherine's teaching, and it provides the framework for her actions in the area of Church reform.

Between the autumn of 1377 and October 1378, Catherine dictated her conversations with God to one, two, and sometimes three scribes simultaneously. During these sessions, she was able to maintain clarity of thought, which allowed her to switch from one topic to the next without difficulty. "*The Dialogue* is chiefly responsible for her title of Doctor of the Church."[58] It is her crowning work, and it is highly regarded as one of the great spiritual classics of all time.

The basic structure of *The Dialogue* consists of four petitions, which Catherine brings to God. With every petition, a discussion ensues, as God responds to her requests. Catherine follows each response with a prayer of thanksgiving. It is through these petitions that Catherine reveals her overriding concern for the salvation of souls, and to this end she begs God for instruction. Catherine's four petitions are: her own spiritual needs; reform of the curia; conversion of the world; and Raymond's spiritual needs.

Note that in the second petition, Catherine pleaded with God for the reform of the Church. In her prayer, she agonized over the failures of God's servants who were supposed to care for the faithful. Her desire was to participate in the healing of the "vineyard of holy Church,"[59] and she asked God to light within his servant, the pope, "a lamp of grace by which he might pursue the Truth."[60]

In order to truly understand Saint Catherine's heartfelt petitions for the Church, we must once again look back at the historical stage of the time. Here we see the dire circumstances that formed the backdrop of people's lives and through which they had to persevere. This was a time of desperation in both the Church and in society, and prayer had an underlying sense of urgency.

As we know, in Catherine's day, there were dangers from within and from without the walls of the Church. Even though the pestilence of the plague came from outside the Church, it took center stage. Not a single person in all of Europe was unaffected. Even though as of this writing the world is still reeling from the global COVID-19 pandemic, it is difficult for us to imagine anything like the plague that shaped Catherine's entire world. Some historians say that this indiscriminate killer had a significant impact on the way in which Catherine dealt with others, especially those in positions of power. As members of the human race, Catherine knew that we are all are susceptible to death, both physically, and more importantly, spiritually. In other words, at the foot of the cross, we are all equal.

This second type of death, the death of the spirit, concerned Saint Catherine in a deep and lasting way. She knew that our spiritual health depends on our relationship with Christ, and that our devotion to his Church nurtures and empowers this relationship. Consequently, the clergy and religious men and women were always at the heart of Catherine's thoughts and prayers. These were the servants to whom God entrusted the spiritual welfare of others, and yet in Catherine's time, they were certainly not immune from the difficulties and dangers that prey upon souls.

Regardless of the risk, many clergy and religious acted as devout angels of mercy, moving among the sick, caring for their needs, and comforting them in their hour of death. As a consequence, many among the religious lost their lives and left the faithful without the tangible expression of Christ's presence and love. As a result of the plague, Europe's population was dwindling, as were the numbers of priests and those choosing to enter the religious life. Unfortunately, the desperate need for priests during this time of suffering and sorrow was unimaginable, and to compensate for this shortage, standards for admission to religious life and holy orders were very low.

Satan can plant seeds of decay even in the sincerest heart of a priest, and this is not a new phenomenon; rather it is simply a continuation of the legacy of sin that haunts the story of mankind. We have only to look at our modern time to see how devastating the consequences are when the leadership of the Church is lacking in discipline and Divine calling. As we might expect, these short-sighted actions have a long-lasting impact on the Church. And in Catherine's day, they were responsible for some of the abuses that she longed to repair. In *The Dialogue*, Catherine shows us an undying love for the universal Church, in spite of the frailties and the sins of her members. Her devotion to the office of Saint Peter is undeniable, and her willingness to put all at risk to uphold its integrity was nothing short of remarkable.

At one point in *The Dialogue*, Catherine asked the Father to reveal the sins of priests to her. Because Saint Catherine's motive was love and not judgment — she wanted only to be stirred to deeper prayers for the souls of the clergy — God granted her request and revealed to her the evil that his ministers were doing. First, though, he reminded Saint Catherine of the sublime dignity of the priesthood and the reverence due to priests by virtue of the sacrament of the altar, which they alone have received the power to celebrate. He told her:

> And if you should ask me why I said that this sin of those who persecute Holy Church is graver than any other sin, and why it is my will that the sins of the clergy should not lessen your reverence for them, this is how I would answer you: Because the reverence you pay to them is not actually paid to them but to me, in virtue of the blood I have entrusted to their ministry. If this were not so, you should pay them as much reverence as to anyone else, and no more. It is this ministry of theirs that dictates that you should reverence them and come to them, not for what they are in themselves, but for the power I have entrusted to them, if you would receive the holy sacraments of the Church. ...
>
> For this reason, no one has excuse to say, "I am doing no harm, nor am I rebelling against holy Church. I am simply acting against the sins of evil pastors." Such persons are deluded, blinded as they are by their own selfishness. ...
>
> Whatever is done to them I count as done to me. For I have said and I say it again: No one is to touch my christs. It is my right to punish them and no one else's.[61]

In essence, the Father is telling Catherine that because of the sacred ministry given to a priest, the sins of a gossiper are worse than the sins of the offender, because what the gossiper says is against God himself.

As their conversation moves further along, we find God and Catherine delving into the idea that God purposely created human beings to need each other in order for each of us to grow in virtue. God tells Catherine:

> I, in my providence did not give to any one person or to each individually the knowledge for doing everything necessary for human life. No, I gave something to one, something else to another, so that each one's need would be a reason to have recourse to the other. So, though you may lose your will for charity because of your wickedness, you will at least be forced by your own need to practice it in action.
>
> Thus, you see the artisan turn to the worker and the worker turn to the artisan: Each has need of the other because neither knows how to do what the other does. So also, the cleric and the religious have need of the layperson, and the layperson of the religious; neither can get along without the other. And so, with everything else.
>
> Could I not have given everyone everything? Of course. But in my providence, I wanted to make each of you dependent on the others, so that you would be forced to exercise charity in action and will at once.[62]

Here God certainly makes an interesting point to Catherine. By telling her that he purposely made all of mankind dependent on one another, he is telling her that our virtues are put to the test by our neighbors. In other words, when someone lacks a particular virtue, or in some cases, has the opposite vice, we have the opportunity to put our own virtues into practice. We recognize this truth from our personal experiences. We also know that the situation gets a little harder when we must be humble in our dealings with the proud, just in the midst of injustice, compassionate to one who is cruel, or kind in the face of someone's wrath. This is when our desire to be charitable must include God's grace. This kind of love is beyond our reach. It is only by grace that God elevates and purifies our love in this way.

Saint Catherine, in her teaching, her writings, and her relationships, tried to live her life in this way of love. And she knew better than anyone that her holiness was dependent upon extraordinary gifts from God. Her holiness did not rest in her mystical experiences, wonderful as they were, but in communicating Christ's love to everyone she met. During her time on earth, she gave everyone she encountered the chance to understand the truth of God's love for us, and the truth of our love for God.

Prayers

Finally, among Catherine's writings we have access to twenty-six of Catherine's prayers, all of which are from the last four years of her life, and most of them from her final seventeen months. As Catherine prayed aloud during these last months of her life, her disciples had the presence of mind to write her prayers down. Along with her letters that were written during this same period, her prayers represent Catherine's spirituality at its most mature.

Reflection Questions

Certainly, we should pray for our priests. They desperately need our prayers. In light of the fact that gossip is a sin, and that God tells Catherine that it is not our place to judge the actions of a wayward priest, how are we supposed to react to the news of then-Cardinal McCarrick, or the many other priests that have been exposed for their heinous acts?

God tells Catherine that he purposely created human beings to need each other in order to grow in virtue. Did the COVID-19 virus affect our ability to reach out to each other? Did it test your ability to grow in virtue?

CATHERINE'S LEGACY

Catherine never abandoned Pope Urban, although he did continue to be a major source of worry. He was supposed to be a shepherd for his people, but he managed to quarrel with nearly everyone he met. In her very last letter to him, written in January 1380, she wrote: "I want to see you governing holy Church and your little sheep so wisely that it will never be necessary to reverse anything your holiness has done or ordained, not even the least word, so that both God and humans may always see a firmness grounded in truth."[63] She hoped that he would stop being so impulsive and that he would soften his heart toward the Roman people, but he would not listen to her advice. That is just the way it was with Urban VI.

It is fair to wonder why Catherine would invest herself so completely in a fairly unstable pontiff. However, it wasn't so much the person of Urban that she was worried about, but the unity of the Church. "For Catherine, the Church was the real focus of her concern; the pope was merely a symbol of its unity — although an essential living symbol: Christ on earth."[64]

On Sunday, January 29, 1380, Catherine suffered a serious stroke, and this proved to be the beginning of the end. In her last letter to Father Raymond, she describes her suffering:

> When Monday evening arrived, I felt a compulsion to write to Christ on earth [the pope] and to three cardinals, so I got someone to help me walk into the study. After I

had written to Christ on earth, I was unable to write any more, so great were the worsening pains in my body. ... The terror and physical pain were such that I wanted to run out of the study and go to the chapel — as if the study had been the source of my sufferings.

So, I got up, and since I could not walk I leaned on my son Barduccio [one of her followers]. But all of a sudden, I was thrown down, and, once down it seemed to me as if my soul had left my body. ... I remained that way for such a very long time that the family was mourning me as dead. By now all the devil's terrors had ceased, and the humble Lamb became present to my soul.

He said, "Have no doubt that I will fulfill your desires and those of my other servants. I want you to see that I am a good master. I act like the potter who smashes and refashions vessels as he pleases. I know how to smash these vessels of mine and refashion them. This is why I am taking the vessel of your body and refashioning it in the garden of holy Church in an entirely new way."

And as that Truth held me close with very winning manners and words (which I pass over), my body began to breathe a bit, and it was evident that my soul had returned to its vessel.[65]

Catherine never fully recovered after this event. By the end of February, she could push her body no more. She was half-paralyzed and frightfully emaciated,[66] and yet, she spent the weeks she had left sharing what she could with her disciples, giving each one a direction to pursue after her death. And she suffered and prayed. In her own way, Catherine felt responsible for the dramatic situation playing out in the Church.

Every day, in spite of her frail health caused by fasting and vigils, Catherine made the daily trip to Saint Peter's Basilica for Mass, sometimes having to drag herself over that long mile. Once there, she prayed for the pope and the universal Church. On April 29, 1380, Catherine finally entered eternal life, in the presence of her spiritual family, including her mother. One of her disciples carried her body to the Dominican church Santa Maria sopra Minerva, where it lay until the evening of the next day. Pope Urban said the Mass with all the ecclesial pomp, and Giovanni Censi, the Senator of Rome, had another Mass said in the name of the Roman people. At long last, the papacy and the city of Rome were in harmony over the death of Saint Catherine.

Over six hundred years after her death, Catherinian scholar Father Thomas McDermott, OP, measured Catherine's life in light of her undying dedication to the Church, and he explains the hope that was within her:

> Humanly speaking, Catherine had more reasons for abandoning the Church than we do today, and yet there is not the slightest indication in her writings that she ever considered doing so. What was the basis of her hope? Undoubtedly, her belief in the human and divine dimensions of the Church undergirded her hope that one day it would be what God intended it to be. In addition, Catherine reported to her confessor and friend Raymond of Capua that the Lord had assured her several times that the Church's "beauty will be restored."
>
> In April 1376, she reported to Raymond a remarkable mystical experience in which the Lord "explained and made clear to me every aspect of the mystery of the persecution the Church is now undergoing and of the renewal and exaltation that is to come. He told me that what is happening now is permitted in order to make the Church once more what she should be." ...
>
> Catherine was told by the Lord that the reform of the

Church will happen with the appointment of new bishops "and other zealous ones." ...

We see another glimpse of Catherine's hopefulness in the midst of so many troubles when she awakens from a mystical experience, in which the Lord had entrusted to her a cross and olive branch to bring to the ends of the earth. Catherine reported to Raymond: "Then I was marvelously happy. I was so confident about the future that it seemed I was already possessing and enjoying it."[67]

Oh, that it may be so!

Saint Catherine of Siena, pray for us!

Reflection Questions

There are many ways in which our lives mirror the circumstances in Catherine's life. In her time, the Church was sharply divided. One might say that we are facing the same situation today. Before she died, however, God told Catherine that the persecution of the Church was necessary, and he assured her that the Church would be renewed and reformed in order to once again be what she should be. In our own day, what would have to happen in order for the Church to blossom once again?

Catherine was deeply rooted in the Christian virtue of hope. Think of an example in her life when this was especially true.

Part Three
Saint Thérèse of Lisieux

*Even now I know it: yes, all my hopes will be fulfilled
… yes … the Lord will work wonders for me which
will surpass infinitely my immeasurable desires.*

WOMAN OF LOVE

As Thérèse lay dying in the Carmel at Lisieux, she overheard a conversation between two of her fellow Carmelites outside her window. They were discussing her obituary, which was to be sent to all of the other Carmels, as was the custom when one of the nuns died. They were wondering aloud what could be said of Thérèse, who was so completely unremarkable. With this, Thérèse smiled to herself because she had been successful in keeping a low profile, which she had long desired.

Truly, her life did seem quite boring. She never traveled, except for a brief trip to Rome when she was fourteen years old. At the age of fifteen she entered the Carmelite cloister, a short walk across town from her home, and she died there nine years later. While she was growing up, Thérèse "played checkers, had a cocker spaniel named Tom whom she loved to take for walks and a favorite blue hat which she thought was ravishing. She wondered how she could love God so deeply and at the same time love that hat so much."[1] In other words, hers was not the life of high adventure. "But in the framework of that life she became a great saint. Therein lies the genius of her message: [Thérèse] teaches us to become holy in the framework of *our* lives, however ordinary they may seem to be."[2] She well understood that "God is in the center of every person's present moment; therefore, no human being is ordinary."[3]

At the time of her death, Thérèse was known only to her family, a few friends, and two dozen nuns with whom she had shared her life in the convent. In fact, fewer than thirty people attended her funeral.[4] Yet today:

> She is known all over the world. She is the only western saint besides St. Francis of Assisi who was popularly revered in Russia during the heyday of communism. Not

even the iron curtain could shut her out of a country avowedly atheistic. People of all races and cultures, of every religion and of none, those with little education and scholars of renown have been fascinated by her. She has been the subject of nine hundred biographies, almost one a month on average, in the [more than] hundred years since her death.[5]

Thérèse has received accolades from every pope in the twentieth century. Pope Pius X, who opened her cause for canonization, called her "the greatest saint of modern times."[6] Pope Benedict XV said of her message: "There is a call to the faithful of every nation, no matter what may be their age, sex or state of life, to enter wholeheartedly upon this way which led Sister Thérèse of the Child Jesus to the summit of heroic virtue ... therein lies the secret of sanctity for all of the faithful scattered over the world."[7] Pope Pius XI canonized her, calling her "the star of my pontificate"[8] and saying, "She gives us an example that everyone can and ought to follow."[9] Pope Saint John XXIII, who made five pilgrimages to her tomb in France, said: "I shall never cease exalting the Great Little Saint."[10] And on Sunday, October 19, 1997, from the balcony overlooking St. Peter's Square, Pope Saint John Paul II proclaimed Saint Thérèse of the Child Jesus and the Holy Face a Doctor of the Universal Church, saying: "Thérèse is a Teacher for our time, which thirsts for living and essential words, for heroic and credible acts of witness."[11]

So, what is to account for this incredible blaze of glory? According to Monsignor Vernon Johnson, a former Anglican priest, now a Catholic priest through the intercession of Saint Thérèse of Lisieux, "It is her littleness and her simplicity. What is most extraordinary about this soul is precisely her extreme simplicity."[12] At the same time, "none of it would have happened if a little fifteen-year-old girl hadn't walked down that street one day and into the Carmelite convent,"[13] full of hope and wonder.

FAMILY LIFE

Before they met and married, Louis and Zélie Martin (who are now saints themselves) had each pursued a religious vocation, only to learn that neither of them was suited for that type of life. God had other plans for them. Those plans began to unfold when Louis the watchmaker and Zélie the lacemaker were married at midnight, on Tuesday, July 13, 1858, "in the splendid church of Notre-Dame in Alençon."[14] At the time, Louis was thirty-five and Zélie was twenty-seven. Fifteen years later, on January 4, 1873, the last child of their marriage, Thérèse, was baptized in the same cathedral. And after another half-century, the statue of the Carmelite nun, beatified on April 29, 1923, then triumphantly canonized in May of 1925, took its place "among those portrayed in stone by the chisels of the sculptors of long ago."[15]

Perhaps as a nod to a certain religious idealism, after their marriage, Louis and Zélie had decided to live together celibately. This lasted about ten months before a good confessor stepped in and advised against this arrangement. Immediately thereafter, Zélie's ambition for many children began to be fulfilled, and they had nine children in thirteen years, seven girls and two boys. Years later, in a letter written to her daughter Pauline, Zélie explained their joy in having children: "We lived only for them. They were all our happiness, and we never found any except in them. In short, nothing was too difficult, and the world was no longer a burden to us. For me, our children were a great compensation, so I wanted to have a lot of them in order to raise them for heaven."[16]

Life and Death in Alençon

The Martins' delight in their children soon turned to shock and sorrow as tragedy relentlessly and mercilessly stalked their little ones. Medicine not being what it is today, infant mortality was a scourge in the second half of the nineteenth century. In fact, "near the end of the nineteenth century, nearly half of the infants born did not survive."[17] This tragedy touched the Martins just as it had so many others. Within a period of three and a half years, they lost two boys and a girl in infancy, and another girl before the age of six. In fact, between 1860 and 1877, Zélie suffered the deaths of both of her parents, her sister, her father-in-law, and four of her children. She was beyond devastated, so much so that she could not even cry. Actually,

> those who did not know Zélie Martin might have thought she was insensitive. When suffering from great shocks, she was incapable of weeping. She mastered her sorrow so well that she attended to her duties as though nothing happened. Only those close to her perceived her interior anguish. … Her relatives were alarmed at this avalanche of troubles that might well destroy her health, which was already uncertain.[18]

Her relatives had reason to worry. For several years, Zélie had been suffering from a tumor in her breast that was getting progressively worse. By the time she tended to the pain, it was too late to even operate. Against the advice of outsiders, who were no doubt whispering, "Eight children, four early deaths, the mother's health endangered … is it not time to stop?"[19], Louis and Zélie's ninth and final child was born at half-past eleven on January 2, 1873. They named her Marie-Françoise-Thérèse. A century later, people around the world would know her as Saint Thérèse of the Child Jesus, often called the Little Flower.

Birth of Thérèse

The series of tragedies only intensified the love of Louis and Zélie Martin for each other. They poured out their affection on their five surviving daughters: Marie, twelve; Pauline, eleven; Léonie nine; Céline, three; and their new-born, Thérèse. The day after her birth, Zélie announced the happy arrival of baby Thérèse in a letter written to her brother and sister-in-law, Isidore and Céline Guérin:

> My little girl was born last night, Thursday, at eleven-thirty. She is very strong and in very good health. They tell me she weighs eight pounds. She seems very sweet. Everyone tells me that she will be beautiful. She already laughs. While I was carrying her, I noticed something that has never happened with my other children — when I sang, she would sing with me. I am confiding this to you. No one would believe it.[20]

Alas, just two weeks later, Zélie followed it up it with another letter to her brother: "I am extremely worried about my little Thérèse. I am afraid she has an intestinal illness. I notice the same alarming symptoms as those of my other children who died. Must I lose this one too?"[21] After two months passed without any improvement, the doctor at last concluded, "This child must be breastfed. That is the only thing that is going to save her."[22] Given her own diagnosis, it was impossible for Zélie to nurse this baby, so it became necessary to give Thérèse to a wet nurse, a peasant woman named Rose Taillé, who had already nursed two of the babies who had died.

Rose lived on the outskirts of Alençon, in a small town named Semallé. Under her care, Thérèse thrived, living the life of a little peasant, spending time outside enjoying the flowers and the animals and all of nature. In this setting, Thérèse grew very attached to Rose, and she "bonded with [her] 'as mother.'"[23] She was with her for just over a year, at which point Rose returned her to the Martin family's brick and stone home at 42 Rue Saint Blaise. To understand Thérèse, it is important to note that before she was eighteen months old, she had twice been separated from the mother figures in her life, namely Zélie and Rose. Being shuffled back and forth in the first year of her life was difficult for her, and she suffered separation anxiety coming and going. Thérèse wanted and needed the security of a permanent mother and a permanent home.

Once she was home, Thérèse quickly became the favorite. Her four sisters smothered her with kisses and tenderness. The affection of her parents for one another and for their children had a profound influence on all of their daughters, evidenced by the love and support that they showed each other. The oldest, Marie, was Thérèse's godmother. In this family of five girls, Marie was the nonconformist, the independent child. Next in line was Pauline, her mother's favorite, and eventually her confidant. Thérèse adored Pauline and held her up as "the ideal." Both Marie and Pauline contributed significantly to Thérèse's psychological and spiritual formation. Léonie, the third, was the child who struggled the most. She was known to be unsociable, rebellious, slow in school, and lacking in good judgment. She was on the periphery of Thérèse's life, as she was the only sister not with her in Carmel, but still she held a special place in Thérèse's heart, and the feeling was mutual. Céline, closest in age to Thérèse, was her constant companion. Thérèse once described Céline as "the sweet echo of my soul."[24]

As a child, Thérèse adored her father, calling him her "King," and in turn, he worshipped her, referring to her as his little "Queen." She asked as much from her mother. By way of an example, Thérèse would call out to Zélie at each step of the stairs as she came down. If Zélie did not respond by saying, "Yes, my little one,"[25] Thérèse would stop and not go any further.[26] Once, in a letter to Pauline, Zélie mentioned that baby Thérèse could be headstrong, claiming "the stubborn streak in her is almost invincible; when she says '*no*' nothing can make her give in, and one could put her in the cellar a whole day and she would sleep there rather than say 'yes.'"[27] At other times, however, she clung to her mother, never wanting to leave her side. Another letter has Zélie confiding in Pauline: "The little one has just placed her hand on my face and kissed me. This poor little thing doesn't want to leave me; she is continually at my side. She likes to go to the garden, but when I am not there, she won't stay but cries till they bring her to me."[28]

Thérèse always wanted things to happen immediately, and by temperament she was an "all or nothing" little girl. A story that has been recounted many times has Léonie offering her two little sisters some pieces of ribbon, yarn, and lace from a small basket, saying, "'Here, my little sisters, *choose*; I'm giving you all this.' Céline stretched out her hand and took a little ball of wool that pleased her. After a moment's reflection, I stretched out mine saying: 'I choose all!' and I took the basket without further ceremony."[29]

In spite of being stubborn and a bit insecure, Thérèse approached life with a genuine sense of spontaneity and joy. "'Full of mischief,' she loved to play tricks on her sisters."[30] Her high spirits delighted the family, and she laughed and enjoyed herself from morning till night, and she sang with all her heart. Physically, she was tall, her hair was blond, and her eyes were a bluish-gray. She had a winning smile, and when she smiled at the world, it smiled back at her. Under the umbrella of love in her family, she matured "quickly, physically, intellectually, and spiritually."[31]

All through their lives, Louis and Zélie remained deeply religious, and they gave their children a solid education in Christian principles. As a family, they spent more time in prayer and less on entertainment. Louis liked to travel and fish, and he was one of the founders of the Catholic Club in Alençon, but for the most part, his life revolved around the home. Twelve years after their marriage, he sold his watch business to his nephew in order to help Zélie with her lacemaking work. Zélie needed the help, as she was busy running her business out of her home, while caring for her husband and family. "They were a unit unto themselves."[32]

The family's preference for a contemplative life led them to being accused of Jansenist tendencies. Jansenists do not believe in a loving God; instead they believe he is a harsh, judging God. Pope Pius XI once called Jansenism "the most insidious of all heresies."[33] At the root of Jansenism is a misrepresentation and distortion of God, "preaching that God was not to be loved as a father, but rather to be feared as an implacable judge."[34] In his book, *The Search for Saint Thérèse*, Peter-Thomas Rohrbach, OCD, explains that it is ludicrous to accuse Saint Thérèse of Jansenism: "Her clear concepts of God's mercy are well known. In fact, she insisted so strongly on God's mercy that some of her statements in the autobiography and in her letters are embarrassing to professional theologians — as, for example, when she said that God has a poor memory because He cannot remember our faults."[35] And where did she learn this? Pope Pius XII tells us that "she learned at her father's knee the treasure of indulgence and compassion contained in the heart of God."[36]

Zélie's Death

Unfortunately, as the days passed, in spite of all their hopes, Zélie's health continued to deteriorate. Knowing that only a miracle could save her, in June 1877, she embarked on a pilgrimage to Lourdes to pray for healing at the Shrine of Our Lady. Marie, Pauline, and Léonie were her companions. Almost nothing went well on the trip, which was full of mishaps of all kinds. And even though she bathed in the icy waters several times and prayed at the grotto, the miracle that Zélie had hoped for did not happen. In fact, the difficult pilgrimage may even have hastened her death. For the next two months, Zélie was in excruciating pain, so much so that she moved to a "remote room in the home so that her sobs could not be heard by the family at night."[37] Ultimately, in the early morning hours of August 28, 1877, Zélie passed away at the age of forty-six. Shortly before she died, she assured Marie and Pauline that they would have no difficulty raising Thérèse, telling them: "Her disposition is so good. She is a chosen spirit."[38] Zélie's maternal instinct had already sensed that "God had laid his hands on Thérèse."[39]

Pauline as "Mama"

Following the funeral Mass, the family maid turned to Céline and Thérèse and said, "Poor little things, you have no mother anymore!"[40] This led Céline to throw her arms around Marie, saying, "You will be my Mama!"[41] Which, in turn, led Thérèse to throw herself into Pauline's arms crying: "Well, as for me, it's Pauline who will be my Mama!"[42] And with that, Thérèse had personally chosen her third mother. She was just four years old. The importance of this exchange between Thérèse and Pauline cannot be overstated. "As Thérèse's life unfolded, Pauline would emerge as the main focus of Thérèse's attention and the major formative influence in her life."[43] Because Pauline played such a prominent role in helping raise her little sister, Thérèse always referred to her as Mother or Mama.

After Zélie died, Thérèse was treated with all the consideration and sympathy due to a young girl who had just lost her mother. Still, no one seemed to realize the profound and lasting effects that her mother's death were to have on Thérèse. In his book, *The Context of Holiness*, Marc Foley, OCD, discusses the psychological reality of this loss on Thérèse before she ever entered Carmel: "There are certain events in life, deaths, births, marriages, divorces, and critical life choices that cut life in two. They determine the 'before' and 'after' for us. They are definitive moments after which life will never be the same."[44] The death of Zélie was such a moment for Thérèse. Forevermore, she "experienced herself as she was *before* her mother's death; how she was *after* her mother died, and how she was when she regained what she had lost *at the time* of her mother's death."[45]

Reflection Questions

Why is it so easy to get labeled (in a negative way), when you are doing something counter-cultural? It happened to the Martins when they were accused of having Jansenist tendencies, and in today's culture, it can easily happen to us. Just expressing an opinion can easily get us labeled a radical of some sort. Why is it so easy to just dismiss people like that? What does that say about us?

What are the "before and after" moments in your life?

LIFE BEFORE CARMEL

Thérèse describes three "before Carmel" periods of her life in her autobiography, *The Story of a Soul*. She tells us that the first period "extends from the dawn of my reason until the departure of our dear Mother for heaven."[46] The second period, she says, is the time after her mother's death until she was fourteen years old, calling those years "the most painful of the three periods."[47] The last period begins while Thérèse is still in her fourteenth year; she was "still subject to much crying, etc., but there [was] a sudden change because of a certain grace she received on Christmas night 1886.

This changed her character completely. She refers to it as her "conversion." Regarding the years in the first period of her life, Thérèse tells us:

> The first is not the least fruitful in memories in spite of its short duration. It extends from the dawn of my reason till our dear Mother's departure for Heaven. God granted me the favor of opening my intelligence at an early age and of imprinting childhood recollections so deeply on my memory that it seems that the things I'm about to recount happened only yesterday.[48]

Period One: Life Before Zélie's Death

The age of reason is the stage in a child's life when he or she can begin to distinguish whether something is morally right or morally wrong, and they can start to make legitimate choices or decisions based on that information. Even though some children experience this earlier or later, it is usually placed around the age of seven. For this reason, it is interesting to note that by the time she was three, Thérèse was already making her own religious decisions and developing her own program of life. In the decree for her beatification, Pope Pius XI claimed that Thérèse "obtained the use of reason when she was barely two years old."[49]

The religious training that Thérèse received from her parents affected her in a deep and powerful way, and it would influence the rest of her life. Shortly before she died at the age of twenty-four, Thérèse confided to her sister, Céline, that "from the age of three, I began to refuse nothing that God asked of me."[50] It is a remarkable statement, yet underneath these words we find the key to Thérèse's life and spirituality. In reviewing her life, there is no evidence of any dramatic decision on her part to live completely for God, "rather it seems that from the dawn of reason she was able, by the grace of God and training that she received at home to make decisions to refuse God nothing she felt he wanted.[51] This must be true because all of the witnesses who testified before her beatification said the same thing: "They had never seen her complete a deliberate, willful fault. There were former schoolmates, teachers, priests, confessors, relatives, nuns in her convent — and their testimony was unanimous: she had lived a completely sinless and blameless life."[52]

On her deathbed, Zélie looked at her sister-in-law, Céline Guérin, the wife of her brother, Isidore, and without words, Céline understood that "Zélie was asking her to take care of her children."[53] This request was taken very seriously. Isidore, now the children's deputy guardian, asked the Martins to move to the Guérins' hometown of Lisieux. They accepted his offer. Louis was heartbroken by Zélie's death; he was fifty-four years old, and he had five daughters to raise. Even though the move amounted to a total uprooting for him, in that his whole life was in Alençon, he sold the lace business and made the move. This began the second period that Thérèse refers to in *The Story of a Soul.* Years later, she remembered that she "experienced no regret whatsoever at leaving Alençon; children are fond of change, and it was with pleasure that I came to Lisieux."[54]

Period Two: "The Most Painful Years of My Life" (Ages Four to Fourteen)

Before the Martin family arrived in Lisieux, Isidore had searched and found a large, red-brick, secluded house close to the Guérins', which the Martins could rent. "It was cloistered by a ring of trees and walls and sequestered on the outskirts of town."[55] The beautiful grounds added to the ambiance. It was a charming place, which the Martin girls christened *Les Buissonnets*, after the little bushes that surrounded the house. It was also adjacent to a spacious park, which was a source of sheer delight for Thérèse. A country girl at heart, deeply nourished by the beauty of nature, Thérèse came home to herself at *Les Buissonnets*.[56] She lived there for eleven years, and it is there that the memories of her childhood took place.

For the most part, the Martin family routine in Lisieux mirrored the life they had left behind in Alençon. At seventeen, Marie took charge of running the house. Sixteen-year-old Pauline helped her and took over the education of the two little ones, especially Thérèse. Léonie, who was fourteen, became a boarder at the Benedictine Abbey in the western section of Lisieux. Céline also went there, but only during the day. The peaceful, bucolic atmosphere that permeated *Les Buissonnets* contrasted with the noisy, urban atmosphere of Alençon, where their home had opened to a busy thoroughfare, with Zélie's workers and customers constantly coming and going. In Alençon, silence and privacy had been a rarity. "At *Les Buissonnets* silence reigned."[57]

Probably "the single most important factor that contributed to the healing atmosphere at *Les Buissonnets* was the predictable availability of Thérèse's father."[58] In Alençon, Louis was focused on running the lace business and taking care of Zélie. In Lisieux, Louis settled into a quiet life comprised of praying, reading, fishing, making pilgrimages, and tending to the needs of his children. Recalling the details of her life, Thérèse tells us that every afternoon after her classes were over (she was taught at home until she was eight), she would take a walk with Papa. They would visit the Blessed Sacrament together, going to a different church every day. During the walk, he would buy her a small gift, and then they would return home together.

This was the essence of life in Lisieux. With the exception of one episode, which is mystifying still today, it was a very ordinary life. In the big picture, this incident might easily have been overlooked, but it was important enough to Thérèse that she included it in her autobiography. In the book, she explains that one day, when her father was out of town on a trip, she was home gazing out at the garden from an upstairs window. Out of nowhere appeared a man who looked just like her father walking toward the bushes. He had the same gait, dress, and general appearance as Louis, but his head was draped in a thick veil, so she was unable to see his face. It was a disturbing sight, and Thérèse cried out to the man, but he suddenly disappeared deep into the bushes and did not come out. Her sisters heard her calling, and they rushed to help her. When she tried to tell them what had happened, they explained that it was not possible, for their father was not due back for several days. However, Thérèse never forgot this event, and in her book, she interpreted this as a prophetic vision of her father's future illness and death.

There were a few other small incidents, but for the most part, her life passed without the sensation of the extraordinary. This highlights an important aspect of Thérèse's life, perhaps the most important, because it makes her so relatable. Thérèse is the saint of the ordinary. In her life, there is no high drama, at least not in the commonly accepted sense of the word. She became a saint by doing ordinary things in an extraordinary way. In fact, in canonizing Saint Thérèse, Pope Pius XI stated: "Thérèse's particular kind of sanctity consisted in readily, generously, and constantly fulfilling her vocation *without going beyond the common order of things.*"[59] Indeed, this is the genius of Thérèse, and it is why so many popes have claimed that she is worthy of our imitation.

From the outside, *Les Buissonnets* appeared to be an ideal place to heal from the many tragedies that had plagued the Martins. On the inside, however, Thérèse was falling apart, which she herself admits:

> My happy disposition completely changed after Mama's death. I, once so full of life, became timid and retiring, sensitive to an excessive degree. One look was enough to reduce me to tears, and the only way I was content was

to be left alone completely. I could not bear the company of strangers and found joy only within the intimacy
of the family.[60]

Thérèse never shed a tear when Zélie died, and she never spoke
of her mother and the memories she had of her. Despite this, the
loss of Zélie was a devastating event in the life of Thérèse, and
ten years would pass before she recovered from it. For her, the
world had become a grim and harsh place, and with the exception of her family, she was emotionally withdrawn and extremely timid. Thérèse referred to these years as her "martyrdom," as
they were years of sadness and weariness and tears, as evidenced
by her excessive sensitivity. Her sister Céline once commented
that she would cry about the least little thing and then she would
cry for having cried.[61]

An interesting observation is that through all of this, Thérèse
did not become a difficult person. Nor did she cease trying to
please God in all things. She continued to pray, attend daily
Mass, perform acts of charity, and offer little sacrifices. Thérèse
intuitively understood that her issues came from within. Basi-
cally, she was a young girl trying to cope in a world that had been
ripped apart because of the death of her mother.[62]

Time for School

In October 1881, at the age of eight, Thérèse replaced Léonie
at the Benedictine Abbey and remained there as a day student
until Christmas, 1885. Thus far, she had been homeschooled
by Marie and Pauline. The Abbey was a typical French convent
school with well-heeled students and unflappable nuns. She was
placed in the fourth, or "green" class, so-called because of the
green sash worn over the uniform. Her homeschooling had born
fruit. Except for writing and arithmetic, Thérèse was at the top
of her class. Consequently, she was placed in a class of girls sev-

eral years older than herself, the eldest being fourteen.

Thérèse had never before socialized with friends outside of her family, and now in her melancholic state, she was overwhelmed by the rowdy nature of her peers in this boarding school environment. Her survival tactic of getting close to people by pleasing them did not work in this situation. She had no experience playing rough and tumble playground games, and no practice in the give and take of childhood banter and teasing. She was also not prepared for the jealousy and bullying that she encountered. In her own eyes, she became what she was in the eyes of others: "boring, awkward, unsociable: an ugly duckling."[63] Sadly, "this ugly duckling in the hen yard was thoroughly pecked at and plucked."[64] And yet, she bore it all without complaint. Thérèse even refrained from telling her family.

It is from this pain that Thérèse discovered that, despite her weaknesses, she had a deep reserve of inner strength, courage, and endurance that she had never tapped into before. But it came with a price. The daily sacrifices placed such a strain on Thérèse that her health gave out. She began to suffer severe and prolonged headaches, the tears flowed more freely, and school became increasingly difficult. Because she kept this situation so close to her heart, no one, particularly Pauline, was expecting what happened next.

Less than a year after she started school, and while that situation was at its most intense, Thérèse overheard Pauline telling Marie that she was going to enter the cloistered Carmelite community in Lisieux. Without knowing exactly what that meant, Thérèse instinctively knew that Pauline was abandoning her. Pauline was leaving all of them just as her mother had left them by dying. With this news, Thérèse shed bitter tears, for she had always dreamed that she and Pauline would forever be inseparable. Later she explained that "it was as if a sword were buried in my heart."[65]

Not knowing the pain that Thérèse was suffering at school, Pauline was surprised by her reaction. She then attempted to comfort Thérèse by describing what her life would be like in a cloistered convent. This talk was crucial, in that Thérèse realized almost instantly that Pauline's vocation was also her own. She tells us that she instinctively knew that Carmel was "the *desert* where God wanted me to go also to hide myself. I felt this with so much force that there wasn't the least doubt in my heart; it was not the dream of a child led astray but the *certitude* of a divine call; I wanted to go to Carmel not for *Pauline's sake* but for *Jesus alone*."[66]

Pauline took Thérèse's desire seriously, so much so that she arranged for her to meet the Prioress, Mother Marie de Gonzague, who listened benevolently as the nine-year-old told her that, like Pauline, she too wanted to join Carmel. Mother confirmed that it was possible for a young girl like Thérèse to have the seeds of a vocation, and she counseled her to continue to nourish this desire until she could enter at the age of sixteen. Thérèse had already imagined that she and Pauline would be able to enter Carmel at the same time, so learning that her dream was not possible was just another heartbreak for the young future saint. In her mind, she had already fantasized about making her first holy Communion on the day of Pauline's clothing, and now she was going home empty-handed, so to speak.

Pauline Enters Carmel

Despite the sorrow felt by the entire family, and most especially by Thérèse, Pauline entered Carmel on October 2, 1882. There were floods of tears, as it was just too much for a young, sensitive Thérèse. Even though the family had been given the privilege of weekly visits, the two or three minutes allotted to Thérèse almost made it worse for her. On top of this was the fact that Pauline was completely happy in the convent, and she wanted nothing else.

For Thérèse, it might have been better if Pauline had just disappeared. The child was in shock, and Pauline's absence reawakened in her "the trauma caused by her mother's death, which had remained latent until then."[67] By the time she reached the age of ten, she had already lost three mothers. In the telling of the story of her soul, she admitted: "The weight of this suffering caused my mind to develop much too quickly, and it was not long before I was seriously ill."[68]

In any case, after Pauline left, Thérèse went back to school. Three months later, around the end of December 1882, her headaches became constant, but she was still able to keep up with her studies, so no one was particularly worried. For the Easter holidays of 1883, Louis took Marie and Léonie to Paris for Holy Week. The two younger girls, Céline and Thérèse, stayed behind with the Guérins. One evening, Uncle Isidore took Thérèse out for a walk, and he proceeded to share memories of his sister, Zélie, and what life was like in Alençon. Suddenly, without warning, Thérèse started to cry uncontrollably. What followed was a complete mental and physical breakdown.

Mysterious Illness

It had been six years since the death of Zélie, and Isidore had no idea that this subject was still such an open wound. He tried to change the subject, but it was too late. "The fit of tears was succeeded by headaches of frightening violence, and in the evening, Thérèse had an attack of shivering resembling fever chills."[69] Aunt Céline put her to bed with warm blankets and hot water bottles, but the trembling continued through the night, and the physician, Dr. Notta, was summoned in the morning. He deduced that she "had a serious illness, and one which had never before attacked a child as young as [Thérèse]."[70] Notta reluctantly diagnosed Thérèse with St. Vitus' dance (chorea),[71] because the symptoms were nearly the same.

Whatever it was, it had taken hold of Thérèse to such a degree that her father thought that she was either going crazy or dying. The next day she had another attack, which was worse than the day before, and by all calculations she was not expected to survive. In her condition, she could not go home, in spite of the fact that her father had rushed back from Paris to care for her. Her symptoms continued for a week, after which "there was a remarkable pause; then the disease entered a new phase."[72]

The date of Pauline's investiture ceremony at the Carmelite Monastery was quickly approaching, and all of the family had planned to go. No one believed in the possibility of Thérèse attending the ceremony, but she assured them that her health would improve, and that is exactly what happened. On the morning of the ceremony, Thérèse arose completely calm and ready to go, as if she was cured. She was not allowed to attend the ceremony, but afterwards, much to her delight, she enjoyed some personal time with Pauline (now called Sister Agnes of Jesus). To the great surprise of her family, Thérèse radiated joy and love the entire day. She returned with her family to *Les Buissonnets* after the ceremony. Despite her assurances that she had been cured, she was sent to bed early.

The next day, she had a serious relapse, and for over a month, Thérèse was confined to bed. During this time, she suffered from hallucinations, comas, and convulsions, among other things. In drawing from original testimonies, Father Peter-Thomas Rohrbach, OCD, details Thérèse's symptoms:

> She appeared to be in delirium, crying out against unseen and terrifying objects. Marie said that she was tossed violently about in bed, hitting her head on the bedboards, as if some strange force were assailing her. Céline observed that these convulsions would sometimes resemble the actions of a gymnastic. Once some

nails on the wall took on the appearance for her of large black fingers and she cried out: "I'm afraid, I'm afraid!" On another occasion her father stood sadly by her bed, his hat in his hands, and Thérèse's eyes fixed on the hat while she cried: "Oh, the black beast!" Léonie remembers that Thérèse would occasionally be thrown out of bed, and one Sunday when the rest of the family was attending high Mass, Léonie remained behind to watch her sister and was witness to one particularly frightening incident: Thérèse had thrown herself on the tile floor and was wedged, head down, between the bed and the wall. Amazingly, she was unhurt.[73]

Her sister, Marie, believed that the convulsive movements of her body were the strangest thing of all. Regarding one particular incident, she says: "She rose up on her knees, and without using her hands, she laid her head on the bed and brought her knees up over her head. And in this position, in which she certainly should have become exposed, she always remained modestly clothed; and it was so astonishing that I can only explain it by attributing it to some heavenly intervention."[74]

Fighting despair, Louis could not help but wonder if his "poor little girl who was like an idiot"[75] was going to live or die. The only time when she exhibited any sense of relief was when she received a letter from Pauline, which she would then read over and over again. The nuns at Carmel joined the entire family in praying for Thérèse. Hoping for a miracle, Louis sent some money for a novena of Masses to be said at Our Lady of Victories Church in Paris. Right in the middle of the novena, Thérèse suffered her worst and final attack, during which she accused Marie of trying to kill her.

Hurt and traumatized, Marie turned to the statute of the Blessed Mother in the bedroom and prayed with fervor for the healing of Thérèse. Léonie and Céline joined her on their knees. Together they begged the Mother of God to secure a miracle for their little sister. Ultimately, Our Lady answered their prayers, and from then on, Thérèse understood that the Blessed Mother was the only mother who would never leave her. She later wrote about her miraculous cure:

> Finding no help on earth ... [I] also turned toward the Mother of Heaven, and prayed with all her heart that she take pity on [me]. All of a sudden, the Blessed Virgin appeared *beautiful* to me, so *beautiful* that never had I seen anything so attractive; her face was suffused with an ineffable benevolence and tenderness, but penetrated to the very depths of my soul was the "*ravishing smile of the Blessed Virgin.*" At that instant, all my pain disappeared, and two large tears glistened on my eyelashes, and flowed down my cheeks silently, but they were tears of unmixed joy.[76]

At last, Thérèse's mysterious illness was over. On May 13, 1883, all of the prayers were answered. And while the cure was instantaneous, her recovery took more time. She was still extremely vulnerable to any form of emotional stress, which caused some minor relapses, but they were nothing compared to what she had previously experienced. In any case, the next day a somewhat weakened Thérèse got out of bed, visited the Guérins, returned to school, and life was restored to normal.

This incident happened over a hundred years ago, yet professionals from a variety of different disciplines still discuss Thérèse's mysterious illness. Everyone seems to agree that the illness represented an eruption of overwhelming anxieties. For those on the outside, Thérèse appeared to have lost her mind. But she claimed this wasn't true:

I said and did things that were not in my mind. I seemed to be almost delirious, saying things that had no meaning. And still I am *sure* that I *was not deprived of the use of my reason for one single instant.* I often appeared to be in a faint, not making the slightest movement, and then I would have permitted anyone to do anything he wished, even to kill me, and yet I heard everything that was said around me and can still remember everything.[77]

So, the question remains: Was it physical, psychological, or spiritual? Dr. Notta was never able to make a concrete diagnosis, but he repeatedly stated: "You may call it whatever you want, but as far as I am concerned it is not hysteria."[78] A more popular diagnosis today would have some believe that she had a nervous breakdown, triggered by the seemingly harmless conversation with her uncle. After all, she was still despondent over her mother's death, she was unhappy at school, and she was in crisis over Pauline's departure for the convent. For her part, Thérèse never deviated from her belief that a demon had overtaken her. She stands by this in her autobiography: "The sickness which overtook me certainly came from the demon; infuriated by [Pauline's] entrance into Carmel, he wanted to take revenge on me for the wrong our family was to do to him in the future."[79]

In contemplating sainthood for Thérèse, Pope Pius XI studied an interesting array of clinical details. He also considered Thérèse's own assertion that her illness was caused by the devil. It was hard to overlook the fact that she maintained complete possession of her interior faculties during the most violent attacks and that she suffered no physical harm from being thrown against the headboard and diving headfirst onto the tile floor. With all of this information, in the decree of beatification, the pope wrote: "She was afflicted with a serious illness whose nature and cure were mysterious; and it was the considered opinion of the family that her sickness was caused by the devil who foresaw the harm she would do him; and that opinion is confirmed by her amazing and sudden cure after special prayers to the Blessed Virgin."[80]

Here it is worth mentioning that immediately after feeling the joy of the Blessed Mother's smile, Thérèse instinctively knew that it was pure grace, and this grace was for her alone. Marie was right there watching it happen, and she later testified to the miracle of it all, saying, "I saw Thérèse all of a sudden staring at the statue; her look was radiant. I understood she was restored, and she was not looking at the image of Mary but at the Blessed Virgin herself. She remained in ecstasy for four or five minutes."[81]

Regrettably, all of the joy found in that moment of grace escaped Thérèse. Out of gratitude for her healing, she shared the miracle with Marie and then reluctantly gave Marie permission to tell the nuns at Carmel. The nuns asked her so many questions, and her answers satisfied them so little, that she began to persuade herself that she had been guilty of lying.[82] In trying to communicate something that was beyond words, the moment became depersonalized, like an event or something out of her past.[83] By telling the nuns, her intimate exchange with the Blessed Mother became nothing but a memory of a grace. In other words, Thérèse revealed a secret that was meant to keep her connected with the eternal, and in doing so, she lost the connection. This was a painful lesson for her, and one that she never forgot.

Adolescence

Almost a year to the day after her miraculous cure, on May 8, 1884, Thérèse received her first Communion. On this, the most "beautiful day of days,"[84] she experienced a new closeness to Christ, a new sense of being loved by him. She cried, but this time her tears were tears of joy. A month later, on Ascension

Thursday, she received Communion for the second time. Soon after, she received her confirmation. In filing through her memories of her first Communion, she later wrote:

> The day after my Communion, I felt born within my heart a *great desire* to suffer, and at the same time the interior assurance that Jesus reserved a great number of crosses for me. I felt myself flooded with consolations so *great* that I look upon them as one of the greatest graces of my life. Suffering became my attraction; it had charms about it which ravished me without my understanding them very well. Up until this time, I had suffered without *loving* suffering, but since this day, I felt a real love for it.[85]

Saying that she was in love with suffering did not mean that she was in love with pain. No, Thérèse was saying that she was in love with *God*, indicating that she was willing to suffer anything out of love for him. Almost without realizing it, she was rooting herself in a spirituality of the "most mature and valid kind."[86]

Her newly declared "love for suffering" was soon challenged when, in May 1885, Thérèse was making her retreat in preparation for the renewal of her first Communion. She was frightened by what the priest (Monsieur l'Abbé Domin) said in his conferences. Her fear was not without merit, as the titles of the conferences were hell, judgment, mortal sin, the necessity of making a good confession, and sacrilegious communion. In one of her letters, Thérèse described this experience: "What [Domin] told us was frightening. He spoke about mortal sin, and he described a soul in the state of sin and how much God hated it."[87] Thérèse's fear triggered an agonizing attack of scruples, which lasted almost a year and a half. In her words:

One would have to push through this martyrdom to understand it well, and for me to understand it well, and for
me to express what I have suffered for a *year and a half*
would be impossible. All of my most simple thoughts
and actions became the cause of trouble for me, and I
had relief only when I told them to Marie. This cost me
dearly, for I believed I was obliged to tell her the absurd
thoughts I had even about her.[88]

Anyone who has ever suffered from scruples knows that it is a
malady of the spiritual life, in which a person experiences extreme anxiety and is overly conscientious about moral issues due
to an unreasonable fear of sin. It is rooted in an image of God as a
harsh judge of unyielding justice. Unfortunately, Thérèse was not
completely cured of scruples after these eighteen months. No, her
tendency toward scruples followed her throughout her life. "The
stern God of Jansenism that gave rise to Thérèse's scruples, which
was in stark contrast to the God of merciful love that Thérèse
experienced at the time of her First Communion, lurked in the
shadows of her mind."[89]

In January 1886, several months into her bout of scruples,
Thérèse was removed from the Abbey because Louis feared that
her ongoing struggle with this would just lead to a relapse of her
illness. So he brought her home and let her finish her schooling
there, with the help of a tutor. Even though she excelled academ-
ically, the years she spent in school would always be remembered
as a time of great suffering for her, and she says as much in her
autobiography: "The five years I spent in school were the saddest
of my life, and if I hadn't had Céline with me, I couldn't have
remained there and would have become sick in a month."[90] All
was not lost, however, for it was in trying to cope with the iso-
lation at school that Thérèse developed a love of reading, which
nourished her heart as well as her mind, and this was something

she relished until the end of her life. Before she entered the convent, she had memorized every word of the *Imitation of Christ* by Thomas à Kempis.

It was in the midst of this schooling change that Marie entered Carmel. Although Marie's leaving was not nearly as traumatic for Thérèse as Pauline's departure had been, it was still painful, nonetheless. Marie had been by Thérèse's side when she received the healing grace from the Blessed Mother. And according to Thérèse, it was Marie who supported her during her struggle with scruples: "[Marie was] the only support of my soul ... she was indispensable to me ... I loved her so much I couldn't live without her."[91] After Marie's departure, Thérèse literally did something she had never done before. She prayed to her four siblings in heaven, asking them to intercede for her:

> I addressed myself to the four angels who had proceeded me there, for I thought that these innocent souls, having never known troubles or fear, would have pity on their poor little sister who was suffering on earth. ... The answer was not long in coming, for soon peace came to inundate my soul with its delightful waves, and I knew then that if I was loved on earth, I was also loved in heaven. Since that moment, my devotion for my little brothers and sisters has grown and I love to hold dialogues with them frequently.[92]

By now, Thérèse was nearly fourteen years old, and although she was no longer a child, she still acted like one. She had been healed of this bout of scruples, but her hypersensitivity remained. Indeed, the overprotectiveness of her family during her childhood was beginning to backfire. She cried over everything. Being dominated by her feelings was not new to Thérèse, but as she grew older, she seemed unable to overcome this. She even wondered how she was going to make it in the adult world of the convent, saying, "I really don't know how I could entertain the thought of entering Carmel when I was still in the *swaddling clothes of a child*! God [will] have to work a little miracle to make me *grow up*."[93] And that is exactly what happened.

It happened on Christmas Day, 1886. On that day, God gave Thérèse the grace to control her "extreme touchiness."[94] She believed that it was the greatest gift that she had ever received, as it restored the part of her soul that she had lost when her mother died. Truly, Thérèse's Christmas miracle cannot be overemphasized. It was *the* event that changed the course of her life, for on this occasion, she "received the grace of leaving childhood."[95]

As the story goes, it was the French custom for the baby of the family to have his or her shoes filled with little gifts on Christmas Day. When the Martin family (Louis, Céline, Léonie,[96] and Thérèse) returned from midnight Mass, Louis noticed Thérèse's shoes near the fireplace and looking at Céline, he groaned, "Thérèse ought to have outgrown all this sort of thing, and I hope this will be the last time."[97] Just then, Céline caught Thérèse's eye and realized that she had overheard that conversation. All too aware of her sister's sensitivity, Céline followed her up the stairs and found her sitting on her bed with tears in her eyes. Céline asked her not to go downstairs in this state. But her concern was baseless, for Thérèse was not the same. At that moment, she had experienced a total conversion. Jesus had completely changed her heart, as evidenced in this passage from her autobiography, *The Story of a Soul*:

> Forcing back my tears, I descended the stairs rapidly; controlling the poundings of my heart, I took my slippers and placed them in front of Papa, and withdrew all of the objects joyfully. I had the happy appearance of a Queen. Having regained his own cheerfulness, Papa was

laughing; Céline believed it was all a *dream*! Fortunately, it was a sweet reality.[98]

Period Three: Free at Last

On that December night so long ago, Thérèse passed a major milestone, which marked the beginning of the third period of her life, "the most beautiful and the most filled with graces from heaven."[99] After nine sad years, she was freed from the faults and imperfections of childhood. The grace she received on that fateful night made her grow up and mature. Her tears dried up, and her excessive sensitivity ended, because God gave her the strength to control it. This was no momentary conquest; rather, it was a radical and lasting change. Céline explained it this way:

> I was a witness to that sudden change and I thought I was in a dream, when, for the first time, I saw her conquer something which would ordinarily have left her desolate. Instead, she began to make my father happy. This change was decisive and never again was she dominated by any sensitivity. That transformation was not limited only to a new self-possession, but at the same time, her soul could be seen to develop and grow in the practice of zeal and charity. She dreamed about the salvation of souls and busied herself, enthusiastically and generously, with the conversion of sinners.[100]

Thérèse maintained that the work that she had been "unable to do in ten years, was done by Jesus in one instant, contenting himself with [her] *good will*, which was never lacking."[101] Spiritual master Blessed Marie-Eugene of the Child Jesus, OCD, tended to agree with Thérèse, claiming that her transformation was not exactly miraculous, but instead it was the result of the Holy Spirit infusing wisdom and bestowing new vigor into her personality, which can happen with souls who are making genuine progress in the spiritual life.[102] After the smile of the Blessed Virgin, the intercession of her little brothers and sisters, and the Christmas conversion, the strong and powerful God had set her free!

As the fruits of Thérèse's conversion unfolded, she began to develop in every area of her life. Her physical and emotional development went hand in hand. She noticeably grew to the point that her cousin called her "tall Thérèse."[103] In addition to her regular schoolwork, she also expanded her love for learning by exploring other disciplines such as science and history. There was also a spiritual awakening in Thérèse. She tells us that she "felt charity enter into [her] soul."[104] She learned anew that freedom is found in looking away from oneself and turning toward the concerns of the other. Subsequently, charity and love became the foundation of her future spiritual "doctrine." By way of an example, Thérèse tells of her experience of going to Mass one Sunday and looking up at Our Lord on the cross:

> I was struck by the blood flowing from one of the divine hands. I felt a great pang of sorrow when thinking of this blood falling to the ground without anyone's hastening to gather it up. I resolved to remain in spirit at the foot of the Cross and to receive the divine dew. I understood I was then to pour it out upon souls. These words ignited within me an unknown and very living fire. I wanted to give my Beloved a drink and I felt myself consumed with a *thirst for souls*. As yet, it was not the souls of priests that attracted me, but those of *great sinners*. I burned with the desire to snatch them from the eternal flames.[105]

The first manifestation of this newborn zeal had Thérèse praying for a murderer named Henri Pranzini. He had been convicted of the brutal killing of three women in Paris, and he was stubbornly unrepentant. She began to pray that this condemned man would make his peace with God, which he had refused to do. Thérèse had but one desire: to save his soul. She ardently prayed and fasted, she had Masses offered, and she even enlisted her sister, Céline, to pray for him. Being that this was her first "case," she asked God for a sign that her prayers were answered. She said very simply: "My God, I am sure you are going to forgive this wretched Pranzini, and I have so much confidence in your mercy that I shall go on being sure even though he does not go to confession, or show any sign at all of being sorry; but because he is *my first sinner*, please just give me one sign to let me know."[106] Her sign came in the form of the morning newspaper, which reported the story of Pranzini's execution and his final act of atonement: He grasped a crucifix and kissed it three times in a gesture of contrition. Overjoyed, Thérèse continued to pray for him for the rest of her life, referring to him as her "first child." Her apostolate of saving souls had begun.

Permission to Enter Carmel

Thérèse's longing to enter Carmel never abated, and it was her hope that she could enter on the first anniversary of her Christmas conversion (December 25, 1887), but she was unsure whether she would be able to secure her father's permission. She was hesitant to ask him because she knew it would demand a great sacrifice on his part. After all, Louis had already lost so much. He had lost four of his children in infancy, his wife had died, his two oldest daughters had entered Carmel, and his daughter Léonie was planning to enter the Visitation convent in July 1887. Plus, he himself had suffered a slight stroke on the first of May, which caused his left side to be paralyzed for hours. And now, on Pentecost Sunday, his youngest daughter, Thérèse, whom he had loved and cared for, was about to deal him the worst blow since the death of his wife.

Thérèse recounts their tender exchange:

> It was in the evening, on coming home from Vespers, that I found my chance. Father was sitting out in the garden with his hands clasped as he drank in nature's loveliness. ... I sat down beside him, not saying a word, but there were tears in my eyes. He looked at me more tenderly than I can express, pressed my head to his heart and said: "What is it, little queen? Tell me." ... Through my tears, I told him about Carmel and my longing to enter soon, and then he too began to weep, but never said a word against my vocation; only that I was still rather young to make such a serious decision. When I insisted, and gave him all of my reasons, his upright, generous heart was soon convinced.[107]

After this exchange, Louis plucked a small white flower, and he gave it to Thérèse. He explained to her how that little white flower symbolized her whole life. God had brought it to blossom and had preserved it until that very day. She tells us that, in listening to her father,

> I believed I was hearing my own story, so great was the resemblance between what Jesus had done for the *little flower* and *little Thérèse*. I accepted it as a relic and noticed that, in gathering it, Papa had pulled all its *roots* out without breaking them. It seemed destined to live on in another soil more fertile than the tender moss where it had spent its first days.[108]

Receiving permission from her father proved to be fairly easy, compared to the host of other obstacles that stood in her way. Her sister Marie was clearly against it, and her Uncle Isidore was adamantly opposed, as was the Prioress Mother Marie de Gonzague. The Carmelite Superior, Canon Delatroëtte, absolutely would not hear of it. According to Thérèse, "He received us coldly. ... Nothing could change his attitude."[109] The truth is that all of their objections were reasonable. She was only fourteen years old, her health was fragile, her spiritual maturity was in question, as was her ability to deal with the austere conditions of Carmel. There were also concerns regarding her capacity to adjust to the challenging environment that existed among the other sisters behind the grille. All very legitimate concerns, but not enough to stop Thérèse and Louis, by now her biggest advocate.

Father and daughter would not rest until they had presented her case to Bishop Hugonin, the Bishop of Bayeux, which they did on October 31, 1887. In preparation for the meeting, Thérèse had donned her best white dress and arranged her hair in a knot on top of her head to make herself look older, a gesture that evoked a winsome smile from the bishop. So, she was naturally disappointed to learn that after pouring her heart out and pleading with him to waive the age limit for entrance into Carmel, Bishop Hugonin was still not convinced, saying only that he would have to consult with Canon Delatroëtte, who had already refused her request. After all of this, Thérèse was still in limbo. Between Thérèse and Louis, it was hard to tell who was more disappointed. It was quite unlike Louis to issue any kind of a threat, but this time, on his way out the door, he casually mentioned the possibility of appealing to the Holy Father.

In fairness to Canon Delatroëtte, who frequently gets labeled as the villain in the retelling of Thérèse's vocation story, he knew firsthand the reality of life in the Carmel. He knew that it required a spiritual and physical hardiness, unlike anything Thérèse had ever known. He also appreciated what a burden it would be for all concerned if a young woman presented herself before she was actually ready. Most of all, he was well aware of the complicated and unstable character of Prioress Marie de Gonzague, who might welcome Thérèse one day and regret it the next. In a very real way, he was trying to protect Thérèse from being hurt and disillusioned.

Pilgrimage to Rome

Three days after meeting with the bishop, Thérèse joined her father and Céline on a pilgrimage to Rome, a trip that had been planned months before, seeming to show Divine Providence at work. This was the first and only time that she had ever stepped foot outside of her native Normandy. Thérèse later reminisced about this trip: "I had a feeling I was approaching the unknown, that great things awaited me out there."[110] She was right, but what awaited Thérèse was not to be found in the churches, shrines, and museums, as one might expect. It was something far greater than that, for it was on this trip that Thérèse experienced a deep inner healing, as well as profound insights into the meaning of her vocation.

The expressed purpose of the pilgrimage was to celebrate the golden jubilee of Pope Leo XIII's ordination to the priesthood, "but its unspoken purpose was to make a political statement."[111] Although the French Revolution had toppled the Church in France from its position of power, the influential pilgrims on this trip spoke for the majority of French Catholics, who were "royalist, hostile to the Republic, and strongly opposed to Freemasonry."[112] Going to Rome to commemorate the pope's jubilee was like waving a banner in support of the Church and the papacy. Ida Gorres, author of *The Hidden Face: A Study of St. Thérèse of Lisieux*, offers us an overview of the political landscape at that time:

The Italian controversies with the Church were a thing

of the recent past. In Catholic circles, indignation over their outcome still raged: Church property had been confiscated, theological faculties at universities had been abolished, many monastic orders and congregations had been dissolved, secular schools and civil marriage instituted. The picture of the Pope as the "Prisoner in the Vatican" was still new and full of pathos. Foreign bishops made a point of sending sizeable bands of pilgrims to Rome from time to time; these were both declarations of loyalty to the Vatican and protest demonstrations against the oppressors of the Church.[113]

Knowing this, it is not surprising that when the pilgrims arrived at the train station in Rome, they were met by protesters shouting, "Down with Leo XIII! Down with the monarchy!"[114]

It probably did not help that aside from the Martins, who had their own reasons for going, "the group was made up almost exclusively of representatives of the old royalist Catholic society of France. The political overtones of the pilgrimage were very plain, and almost the entire Norman nobility was present."[115] For them, the pilgrimage was not only an act of piety toward the Holy Father, it was also an excursion for the rich, albeit with religious overtones. The whole affair had the air of being an extraordinary social event, and so it attracted people who cared for that kind of thing. Of particular note is the fact that seventy-five of the total one hundred and ninety-seven pilgrims were priests.

Prior to joining their fellow pilgrims, the Martins spent two days touring Paris on their own. They visited the Louvre, the Bastille, the Royal Palace and other tourist spots, but the highlight for Thérèse was a visit to an obscure church named Our Lady of Victories. Four years earlier, when Thérèse was bedridden, Louis had sent a donation to this church with a request that a novena of Masses be offered for her healing. Before the end of that nine-day novena, while praying with her sisters before the statue of the Blessed Virgin Mary, she was cured. In light of this, it is understandable that Thérèse would want to visit this very same church in order to render due thanks to God for her healing.

There was also another reason why Thérèse wanted to visit this shrine. Recall that she had told Marie and the nuns at Carmel about her experience of that intimate moment of grace between Our Lady and herself. Immediately thereafter, she was sure that she had betrayed a secret between Our Lady and herself. What followed then was a deep sense of guilt. Now here she was four years later, once again on her knees before the statue of the Blessed Virgin, when Our Lady bestowed another healing grace upon her. Thérèse's original feeling of horror finally vanished, and she experienced the true intimacy of Mary's maternal presence. The closeness was so profound that the emotional healing that ensued was as miraculous as the cure had been four years earlier. "I understood she was watching over me, that I was *her* child. I could no longer give her any other name but 'Mama.'"[116]

After their arrival in Rome, they had six days of sightseeing before attending the November 20, 1887, Sunday Mass, which was then followed by an audience with Pope Leo XIII. The time spent sightseeing exposed Thérèse to the lives of the rich and famous, and she was not impressed with their overall sense of shallowness and superficiality. "Ah! far from dazzling us, all these titles ... appeared to us as nothing but smoke. From a distance, this had sometimes thrown a little powder in my eyes, but close up I saw that 'all that glistens is not gold.'"[117] During this time, Thérèse's eyes were also opened to the worldliness of priests who hobnobbed with the wealthy. From a distance, they appeared to her to be "as pure as crystal," but up close, she saw them as "weak and fragile men."[118] This trip certainly highlighted what was to be the essence of her vocation. From then on, she knew that God was calling her from the world to pray and suffer for sinners, and most especially, to pray for priests. Up until that time, the reason for her vocation was a mystery to her. Now she knew, and she well understood that this mission would require her to mount the cross that awaited her.

Thérèse's main purpose for going to Rome was to obtain permission from Pope Leo XIII to enter Carmel at the age of fifteen, as all of her other possibilities had been exhausted. It should be noted that Thérèse's decision to address the pope was not an impulsive one. The plan had actually been devised by Mother Marie de Gonzague (who had changed her mind about Thérèse's date of entry), in conjunction with members of her own family. However, when Pope Leo XIII sat down on his throne to receive the pilgrims, her confidence began to waver, particularly since the group had been given a firm warning not to speak to him. Despite this, she simply could not let this moment pass, so she turned to Céline for advice: "'Speak!' she said."[119] Thérèse tells us that a moment later:

> I was at the Holy Father's feet. I kissed his slipper and he presented his hand, but instead of kissing it I joined my own and lifting tear-filled eyes to his face, I cried out: "Most Holy Father, I have a great favor to ask of you!"
>
> The Sovereign Pontiff lowered his head toward me in such a way that my face almost touched his, and I saw his eyes, *black and deep*, fixed on me and they seem to penetrate to the depths of my soul. "Holy Father, in honor of your Jubilee, permit me to enter Carmel at the age of fifteen."[120]

In a hushed tone, the pope told Thérèse to follow her superiors, saying "Go … go … *You will enter if God wills it.*"[121] Heartbroken, Thérèse left the meeting in tears, but this time she tells us that she "felt a great peace, since I had done everything in my power to answer what God was asking of me."[122] She knew that she would enter Carmel when and if God willed it. And yet, "she never ceased hoping against all hope."[123]

Some have accused Thérèse of disobedience in light of the fact that she reached out to the pope after being forbidden to do so. Others have claimed that she was just being obstinate. However, Pope Leo XIII's successors all seem impressed by the courage she displayed. After all, she was a fourteen-year-old girl from the provinces on her first journey outside of Normandy, and she was thrust into an audience with the Holy Father. "It entailed no small amount of courage for the young Norman girl to marshal her resources for a direct appeal to the white-frocked figure on the Papal throne."[124]

Thérèse arrived back in Lisieux on December 2, 1887, but she heard nothing about her application until after Christmas, and even then, there was a catch. She was accepted, but she would have to wait until April 9, 1888, before entering Carmel. At first, she confessed to the temptation to relax during this time, but she quickly dismissed that idea in favor of performing sacrificial acts every day. She tells us that these sacrifices "consisted in breaking my will, always so ready to impose itself on others, in holding back a reply, in rendering little services without any recognition, in not leaning my back against a support when seated, etc., etc."[125] It was through the exercise of these "nothings" that she prepared herself to become the fiancée of Jesus. All in all, this time turned out to be a blessed time for Thérèse.

Reflection Questions

Have you ever received a grace that completely changed the way you approach life, as Thérèse did on Christmas Eve, 1886?

Some things are meant only for us; they are not meant to be shared. For example, when Thérèse shared her secret about her intense connection with the Blessed Mother with Marie, and then Marie told her fellow sisters, Thérèse immediately knew that she had lost the connection. This was an extremely painful lesson and one that she never forgot. Has anything like this ever happened to you?

What is the significance of Thérèse's point in *The Story of a Soul* when she writes of Louis pulling out all the roots of the little white flower without breaking them?

THÉRÈSE, THE CARMELITE

The time passed very quickly, and the day finally arrived. Thérèse is the only person who could do justice in telling the story of her farewell:

> On the morning of the great day, casting a last look upon *Les Buissonnets,* that beautiful cradle of my childhood which I was never to see again, I left on my dear King's arm to climb Mount Carmel. As on the evening before, the whole family was reunited to hear Holy Mass and receive Communion. As soon as Jesus descended into the hearts of my relatives, I heard nothing around me but sobs. I was the only one who didn't shed any tears, but my heart was beating *so violently* it seemed impossible to walk when they signaled for me to come to the enclosure door. I advanced, however, asking myself whether I was going to die because of the beating of my heart. Ah! What a moment this was! One would have to experience to know what it is. ...
>
> After embracing all of the members of the family, I knelt down before my matchless Father for his blessing,

and to give it to me he placed *himself on his knees* and blessed me, tears flowing down his cheeks. It was a spectacle to make the angels smile, the spectacle of an old man presenting his child, still in the springtime of life, to the Lord! [126]

Once the doors of the Carmel closed, she tells us that her desires were finally fulfilled and that her soul had experienced a "*PEACE*, so sweet, so deep, it would be impossible to express it."[127] Even in the midst of her greatest trials, that inner peace of soul stayed with her until the day she died, eight years later.

That said, the Carmel at Lisieux was a far cry from what Saint Teresa of Ávila had in mind when she began her reform. When she established her first convent, the Spanish foundress insisted that "In this house where there are no more than thirteen — nor must there be any more — all must be friends, all must be loved, all must be held dear, all must be helped."[128] Saint Teresa was full of common sense when she laid down a balanced way of life that had love taking precedence over everything else. Three centuries later, that original vision of "love above all" had been lost, as some of the Carmels had chosen to prioritize different ascetical practices, such as extreme denial or extreme mortification. The Lisieux Carmel had not escaped these tendencies, which the general climate of French Christianity — with its Jansenist leanings — encouraged. And yet, Thérèse tells us that she "found religious life to be *exactly* as I imagined it,"[129] in spite of the fact that her first steps were "met with more thorns than roses."[130]

The first trial that she encountered in Carmel was the makeup of the community. Between Thérèse and the majority of the nuns, "there were such differences in temperament, social background, and everyday behavior!"[131] Most of the nuns had very little education, and they lacked the social graces, as well as the mental aptitude that were part of the culture in which Thérèse was raised. Consequently, she found their lack of judgment, good manners, and temperament hard to endure. "In short, we might say, that Thérèse, who was raised in an upper middle-class bourgeois culture, now found herself living in a 'blue collar' neighborhood."[132]

In turn, there was a real contrast between Thérèse's understanding and that of the majority regarding the matter of work. She definitely did not have domestic skills, and she was unaccustomed to doing simple household tasks. When it came to sewing and sweeping, her two main tasks, she was very slow and awkward. One of the nuns (Sister Saint Vincent de Paul) nicknamed Thérèse "the big nanny goat"[133] because of her slowness when it came to manual labor. She told Mother Marie de Gonzague, who at that time was both prioress and novice mistress, that Thérèse would never be of use to the community. Once, when Thérèse entered the laundry room, the same nun proclaimed, "Here she comes! She is certainly in no hurry! When is she going to get to work?"[134]

The next challenge that Thérèse faced in Carmel came directly from her blood sisters, Pauline and Marie. The two women who had mothered her as a child found themselves mothering her again. They were particularly defensive of her when she was being bullied by the older nuns. Even though she resisted their affections, Thérèse found it very difficult to do so because her desire to be nurtured was very strong. She later claimed that living with her sisters was the cause of continual suffering because she was determined to resist her natural inclinations.

It was not surprising because she had been forewarned, but another test came directly from Mother Marie de Gonzague, the one person who made it possible for Thérèse to enter Carmel. Prior to her entry, Mother Marie had treated her kindly. But her kindness took a different turn after Thérèse became a postulant. Perhaps it was a case of "tough love" overdone, but as a postulant and as a novice, Thérèse received rejections and corrections day after day. She was scolded for being slow at work and inattentive at community prayer. Once, when she missed a cobweb in the cloister, the Prioress raised her voice so that all could hear: "It is easy enough to see that our corridors are swept by a child of fifteen. Sweep out that cobweb and be more careful in the future."[135]

As painful as it was not to let her blood sisters nurture and care for her, it was nothing compared to what she had to endure regarding her father's illness. On June 23, 1888, two months after Thérèse entered Carmel, her beloved father suddenly disappeared from *Les Buissonnets*. When they found him four days later in the city of Le Havre, about an hour away from Lisieux, he explained that he wanted to live as a hermit. Louis' mental confusion was the result of physical and emotional factors. He was suffering from heart disease and a kidney infection, and he was also mourning the loss of his children. Thérèse had entered Carmel on April 9, 1888, and on June 15, Céline informed her father of her desire to do the same. At the time, Léonie was also making plans to reenter the Visitation at Caen. It is understandable that he was despondent over the fact that all of his children were abandoning him. As each day passed, he became more unstable, and it was questionable whether or not he would be able to attend Thérèse's clothing ceremony on January 10, 1889. And yet, to the surprise of everyone, he was there.

But it was just a matter of weeks before Louis became delusional. He heard strange sounds and screams, and he began to carry a revolver in order to defend his family. His brother-in-law, Isidore Guérin, the man who had stood by him for so many years, was forced to institutionalize him in Bon Sauveur mental asylum in Caen on February 12, 1889. This was almost more than Thérèse could bear. When she made her final commitment in September 1890, she had hoped that her father would be able to attend, but that hope was never realized. However, her Uncle Isidore did bring Louis back to Lisieux on May 10, 1892, for a short visit. This was the last time she ever saw her "King." Once so dignified and handsome, Louis was now gaunt, and he had lost most of his faculties. He was almost mute, and when he did speak, he did so only in phrases, "My little queen, etc." He left in tears, pointing upwards to heaven. Sadly, he lived in this state for two more years and finally died on July 29, 1894.

Daily Routine

After Thérèse's final vow celebration, daily life returned. From that day forward, Thérèse wore the Carmelite habit: "rough homespun and brown scapular, white wimple and veil, leather belt with rosary, woolen stockings, rope sandals."[136] But there was one very significant change. She began signing her name Sister Thérèse of the Child Jesus *of the Holy Face*,[137] which symbolized Christ's suffering, a devotion she had carried forward from her childhood into Carmel. This devotion had been a tremendous comfort to her during her nearly nine years in the convent, and it was the force behind her doctrine of the Little Way. Before we shine light on this, it will be helpful to look at her daily routine:

> The daily life of the Lisieux Carmelite convent began with rising at 5:00am (6:00am in the winter). A wooden clapper awakened the Sisters. There was an hour of mental prayer, followed by Mass and the Liturgy of the Hours. Breakfast was bread and coffee, followed by a work period that ended at 11:00, when the main meal was served. After the meal the Sisters had an hour for recreation, when they were officially allowed to talk. Vespers started at 2:00pm, then spiritual reading and a second hour of mental prayer at 5:00pm. After a light dinner and a second recreation period, Compline was said at 7:30pm. Matins and Lauds were chanted at 9:00pm, and the nuns retired around 11:00.[138]

Just glancing at the schedule and thinking about living within the walls of a convent and a garden enclosure, with no outside entertainment or trips, with the same group of twenty or twenty-five women, day by day, year after year, highlights the fact that this was a life of sacrifice, with great demands on the human spirit.

The Little Way

Thérèse might not have been good with a broom, but she was a master in understanding the human condition. As we can see, she did not live with angelic beings who had been left unscathed by the brokenness of this world. Several of the nuns were difficult to live with, a few of them were emotionally disturbed, and one had to be institutionalized. Thérèse had to find a way to deal with it. Her way was love. In fact, she once exclaimed, "My Vocation is Love!"[139] She learned to love people as they were, not as she wanted them to be. This is what she called her Little Way, and it was her own means to holiness. Joseph F. Schmidt, FSC, author of *Everything is Grace: The Life and Way of Thérèse of Lisieux*, tells us about Thérèse's Little Way:

> [It] is an attitude, a disposition of heart, a way of awareness and willingness. It is a way of accepting and reciprocating God's love, available in all of life's experiences. It is a way of responding, under the impulse of the Spirit, to divine love with confidence, abandonment, and trust, sharing that love with others in justice and peace. ... [it] does not require a prior attachment of a degree of perfection to receive God's free and merciful love, but requires only, within our human condition of weakness, a spirit of abandonment and a willingness to receive and share that love.[140]

Following the Little Way of Saint Thérèse helps us to understand that we can all weave a tapestry of hope from the threads of everyday life. Everything we do is precious, if we do it out of love for God.

Death: The Ultimate Trial of Faith

Saint Thérèse's final transforming union with the suffering Christ began on the night between Holy Thursday and Good Friday 1896. In her own words, she describes what happened: "I returned to our cell [shortly after midnight], but I had scarcely laid my head upon the pillow when I felt something like a bubbling stream mounting on my lips. I didn't know what it was, but I thought perhaps I was going to die and my soul was filled with joy. ... It seemed to me that it was blood I had coughed up."[141] It was blood indeed, which she verified in the morning. The diagnosis was tuberculosis. Thérèse told Mother Marie de Gonzague, but begged for no special attention. Thérèse was not frightened; just the opposite. She hoped soon to be with the One she loved in heaven. But during the joyful Easter season,

> Jesus made me feel that there really were souls who have no faith, and who, through the abuse of grace, lost this precious treasure, the source of the only real and pure joys. He permitted my soul to be invaded by the thickest darkness, and that the thought of Heaven, up until then so sweet to me, be no longer anything but the cause of struggle and torment.[142]

This great trial of faith lasted her entire illness. Her last year and a half of increasingly severe bodily pain was overshadowed by the cloud that obscured the joy of faith. She compared it to traveling through a dark tunnel. When she tried to get a glimpse of that land she had pictured and longed for, it seemed that the darkness grew thicker. As each day passed, the sufferings increased. She could no longer retain food, her fevers persisted, as did her feelings of suffocation. There were days that she could not even bear the slightest noise or movement around her. It hurt her to hear someone talk about heaven. It seemed that as each day drew darker, her love for Christ increased. The darker the day, the greater the love. The physical suffering was so intense that on the day she died, she said to her sisters, "Never would I have believed it was possible to suffer so much! Never! Never! I can't explain this except for the ardent desires I have had to save souls!"[143] And still, at the moment of her death, she looked at her crucifix one last time, and said, "Oh! I love Him! ... My God, I love You!"[144] And with that, at 7:20 p.m. on September 30, 1897, she closed her eyes.

THÉRÈSE'S WRITINGS

During her life, Thérèse wrote letters, poetry, prayers, plays, and all other forms of correspondence. However, *The Story of a Soul* is Thérèse's principal work and the main source of our knowledge of her. It is not an autobiography in the traditional sense, although it has continued to be labeled as such. Rather, it is more in the genre of Saint Augustine's *Confessions*, in that it is Thérèse's thoughts regarding the graces that God had deigned to give her.

In reality, the *Story of a Soul* is made up of three distinct manuscripts written over the course of the last two and a half years of her life. It was only out of obedience to her superiors that Thérèse agreed to this project. She wrote Manuscript "A," the longest of the three, over the course of 1895. It is a composition of her childhood memories, which speaks of the manifestation of God's merciful love in her life. Manuscript "B," written in September 1896, is an explanation of her Little Way of spiritual childhood. Many believe that this is the most beautiful section of the book because it contains so many of her spiritual insights. Thérèse wrote Manuscript "C," about her religious life, while she was on her deathbed. She wrote until she could literally write no more. She actually terminated the manuscript in the middle of a sentence.

It was while writing Manuscript C that Saint Thérèse came to understand that there was a hidden, Divine plan for her future. Only then did she come to know and to prophesy about her future mission of helping from heaven. At that time, she perceived that through the publication of the book many people would come to know, love, and serve God. She entrusted the work of editing and revising the manuscripts for publication to Mother Agnes.

Less than two months before she died, Thérèse expressed her desire for the text to be published as soon as possible after her death. She sensed that the world, at the brink of the twentieth century, needed to hear the story of her experience of God's mercy. Thérèse also sensed that if it wasn't published immediately, Satan would try to destroy the work. She told Mother Agnes: "After my death, you mustn't speak to anyone about my manuscript before it is published. You may speak about it only to Mother Prioress. If you act otherwise, the devil will make use of more than one trap to hinder the work of God, a very important work!"[145]

THÉRÈSE'S LEGACY

Shortly after Thérèse's death, Mother Marie de Gonzague gave her permission to publish the manuscript. On September 30, 1898, the first anniversary of her death, Thérèse's *The Story of a Soul* was ready for distribution. Instead of sending out the usual obituary, in October, 1898, Mother Marie de Gonzague arranged to have 2,000 copies of Thérèse book (with an added account of her death) sent to Carmelite convents throughout the world. Its effect was electrifying — first among the Carmelites, then as it was reprinted and translated many times, among millions of others who were introduced to Thérèse's Little Way of spiritual childhood. "The simple message of the spiritual journal bolted through the Church like a flash of lightening."[146]

Before she died, Thérèse had a feeling that her activity after death would extend far beyond the influence of the book. In fact, she had a premonition that she would be known all over the world. This intuition led her to make her now famous prediction: "I feel that my mission is about to begin, my mission of making others love God as I love him, my mission of teaching my little way to souls. If God answers my requests, my heaven will be spent on earth up until the end of the world. Yes, I want to spend my heaven in doing good on earth."[147] Since her death, all of the evidence points to the fact that she has done exactly that. For today, "there is no moment of any day in which someone does not turn to her. And pilgrims pass before her tomb in an endless stream. She is 'the child loved by all the world.'"[148]

Thérèse never founded a new convent, reformed a religious order, or brought the pope back to Rome, so why do so many people turn to her seeking hope and guidance for the big and small decisions of their lives? In other words, what is it about her that is so appealing? As mentioned earlier, it is her simplicity. She speaks our language. We can hope because she hoped. In spite of all of the obstacles that came her way, Thérèse never gave up! And for those who turn to her for help, she makes life easier. There is a well-known story regarding Pope Pius X and Thérèse, and it goes something like this: "One day a priest said to Pius X that there was nothing extraordinary in the life of Thérèse, to which the Pope replied, 'What is most extraordinary about this soul is precisely her extreme simplicity. Consult your theology.'"[149]

Saint Thérèse of Lisieux, pray for us!

Reflection Questions

What role did suffering play in Thérèse's life?

Why did Thérèse want her book published as soon as possible after her death?

Thérèse was deeply rooted in the Christian virtue of hope. Think of an example in her life when this was especially true.

Part Four
Saint Hildegard of Bingen

*Spare those who sin, O loving Father! You
have not forsaken the exiles, but have raised
them up upon Your shoulders. And so we
do not perish, who have hope in You.*

WOMAN OF CONSEQUENCE

Presuming that Rome has eternity on its side, a span of 800 years is not a long time. Still, it was a long time for Saint Hildegard. It took over eight hundred years and five popes, beginning with Pope Gregory IX and ending with Pope Benedict XVI, to officially recognize her as the saint she is, but at long last, it happened. On May 10, 2012, Pope Benedict XVI "acknowledged her as a saint through his authority and through a process known as equivalent canonization — that is, she had been venerated for centuries but never officially canonized."[1] Five months later, on October 7, 2012, he publicly declared Hildegard of Bingen a Doctor of the Church, the fourth woman to be so named. She was honored for "the clarity of her teachings, her love of the Church, and especially her obedience to the Church's authority."[2]

Hildegard's Benedictine sisters tell her story a bit differently. Mother Superior Clementia Killewald, OSB (now deceased), agreed that, indeed, "it took seven campaigns and five popes to conclude Hildegard's cause."[3] To which she wryly added, "It also took 39 abbesses and 39 generations of sisters from the monasteries of Rupertsberg and Eibingen, both founded by Hildegard, who 'prayed for this and exerted themselves tirelessly up to our own days' to make it happen."[4]

Long before Hildegard died, she had been revered as a saint, and for centuries, she was known as Saint Hildegard, particularly in Germany, the country of her birth. The fact that she had never been formally canonized mattered little. As time passed, however, she nearly fell into obscurity, "even in the diocese of Mainz and the town of Bingen."[5] It seemed that Hildegard might be lost to the ages. Thankfully, this all began to change in the late nineteenth century with the rediscovery of Hildegard's music by the monks of Solesmes in France.

The Hildegard revival took hold of the English-speaking

world in the second half of the twentieth century. It was then that Latin and medieval scholars began translating her writings from Latin into English. It was an exceptionally difficult task, given that she had never actually mastered the ins and outs of Latin grammar. While many of the exact details of Hildegard's life are still in question (dates, places, etc.), the dedication of these scholars paid off in that they were able to bring Hildegard out from the shadows and into the light. Without them, it is doubtful that she would have become a Doctor of the Church.

Others may have forgotten Hildegard, but Pope Benedict XVI, the first German pontiff since the Middle Ages, had not. They shared a common homeland, after all. But if that was all it was, Benedict could easily have chosen to give the title Doctor of the Church to Edith Stein (Saint Teresa Benedicta of the Cross), the twentieth-century Carmelite philosopher who died in Auschwitz, which would have been a logical choice. With Hildegard, there was something more, even though from the outside, it seemed that Hildegard and Benedict were a mismatch — he the caricature of arch-conservatism and she the caricature and icon of secular feminism.

Yet they had more in common than one might think. The corruption and the abuse of power within the Church "deeply affected both Ratzinger [Pope Benedict XVI] and Hildegard as they developed prophetic outlooks on the nature of the Church and its mission in the world."[6] In Hildegard, Pope Benedict found a soulmate, and he "called upon her to help shape his visions for Church reform."[7] In fact, Pope Benedict quoted Hildegard directly several times when speaking about the disfigurement of the Church, due to the many scandals that had engulfed her. For example, in his 2010 Christmas greetings to members of the curia, Pope Benedict cited Hildegard in the context of the Catholic Church's recent sex abuse scandal, saying: "In the vision of St. Hildegard, the face of the Church is stained with dust ... Her garment is torn — by the sins of priests. The way she saw it and expressed it is the way we have experienced it this year."[8]

Neither Hildegard nor Benedict were afraid to call the abuse for what it was: pure evil. Most importantly, however, is the fact that neither dared to put their trust in human institutions to fix these problems. Instead, they both looked to the "gleaming hope of redemption offered by the Incarnation"[9] — that is, Jesus Christ.

No woman of the Middle Ages was more accomplished or more renowned than Saint Hildegard of Bingen. In addition to being a first-class theologian and philosopher, Hildegard was a "medieval chemist, botanist, naturalist, poet, hymnist, mystic, abbess and saint."[10] Not only was she a remarkable Catholic leader, some historians claim that she was the most powerful woman of her era. Hildegard was strong, assertive, and confident. As if to prove that there was nothing she could not do, this holy woman lived to be eighty-one years old, when the life expectancy at that time was mid-thirties. In our day and age, it is difficult to comprehend the breadth of her accomplishments.

HILDEGARD'S EARLY YEARS

Born in the summer of 1098, Hildegard was the tenth and last child of a German noble family in the Rhineland town of Bermersheim, near Alzey, southwest of Mainz. Her parents were Hildebert and Mechtilde; her father was a soldier for the Count of Sponheim, and her mother was a noblewoman. At birth, her parents promised her as a "tithe" to the Church, which was a "tradition but by no means an obligation concerning the tenth child."[11] This practice, also called an oblation, was popular among well-to-do religious families, even those who had fewer children. It is worth noting that later in her life Hildegard objected to the forced dedication of children to the religious life at such a young age.

Hildegard lived in the beautiful Rhine River valley, which is the wine-growing region of western Germany known as Rheinhassen. The Middle Rhineland[12] valley is one of the most fertile parts of Germany, with a mild, temperate climate, where people have lived in communities for ages. As a matter of fact, Heinrich Schipperges, author of *The World of Hildegard of Bingen*, tells us:

> Hildegard spent her entire life in the perspective of this fundamentally agricultural society: as a girl in her parents' holding; as an enlightened nun in the land of Disibodenberg and Rupertsberg monasteries; as a responsible abbess riding along the lanes and roads of Germany not only to carry out her formal duties, but on preaching tours as a sought-after consultant to emperors and popes as the "Rhineland prophetess," or Sybil; and as "the jewel of Bingen" bringing illumination to very different parts of Europe.[13]

In 1099, when Hildegard was just a year old, Jerusalem was rescued by the Christians. During her long life, she lived through both the First and Second Crusades, as well as papal schisms and powerful temporal rulers vying for, and warring over, power.[14] Be that as it may, the twelfth century gave rise to a new and astonishingly rich and complex world. It is safe to say that "every facet of life was subject to reform, examination, classification, and evolution."[15] From the start, it was the highpoint of the period known as the High Middle Ages. In her book entitled *Hildegard of Bingen: The Women of Her Age*, Fiona Maddocks gives us a glimpse of life in Germany during the twelfth century:

> Trade was thriving. Great mercantile routes crisscrossed Europe, bringing grain, wax, honey, wood and furs from

the east; silk, damask, porcelain and ivory from the south. The Rhine linked the important commercial areas of Flanders and the Rhine delta to the Lombard cities south of the Alps. Trade companies and guilds emerged. Methods of travel and navigation were improving; maps grew more sophisticated; the compass, borrowed from the Chinese, came into use; technical refinements to sailing eased hazardous sea voyages. ...

[Still] those people with trades — bakers, millers, goldsmiths — maintained their smallholdings and vineyards and grew much of their own food, fearful of renouncing all links with the land because of uncertainty about their urban future. The agrarian landscape, too, had changed. New crop systems and better tools led to improved harvests. Reclaimed land was used for growing cereals, pulses and root vegetables, a stable diet, supplemented by fifty kinds of fresh water fish. Meat from livestock, mainly salted, was eaten in moderation, less frequently than game.

Houses, usually made of timber, were dark, damp and cramped, with earthen floors and low, narrow doors. Homes of the gentry, to which Hildegard's family belonged, might have exotic textiles and wall hangings brought back from the Crusades, but most people relied on wool and linen of the homeliest varieties.[16]

Because of the many dramatic changes, this time period has been loosely termed the "Renaissance of the twelfth century."[17] It was the beginning of an enormous shift in the Church, as it was the time of "two great theological movements that have had a profound influence on the Church to this day: the ancient monastic contemplative tradition; and the dawn of the new and revolutionary development of Scholastic theology."[18] Even though

Hildegard was firmly rooted in the monastic tradition, and even though she did not live to see the flowering of Scholasticism, she was aware of this new theological stream.[19]

The changes of the twelfth century were not limited to the theological arena, however, as this was also a century of widespread cultural and ecclesial malaise. The State was encroaching ever more into the affairs of the Church. The clergy were indolent and ineffective, often corrupt and unchaste; the laity were poorly catechized; and the Church was at risk of destruction by heretics.[20] There was an air of anxiety and uncertainty and a longing for the predictable. Years later, in a vision, "Hildegard was to recall the time of her birth as a moment of great unrest."[21]

Little is known about Hildegard's younger years, other than the fact that her spiritual gifts (visions, prophesies, etc.) began to emerge quite early. Hildegard's biography puts this as far back as when she first learned to talk, claiming that she spoke of her visions naturally until her fifteenth year, only gradually realizing that others did not see as she did.[22] It was through these early visions that Hildegard came to know the utterly incomprehensible God, whom she referred to until her dying day as the "Living Light." But once she became aware of how different she was, she mostly kept these things to herself until she was an adult.

Only one of her earliest visions was recounted in her canonization testimony. When Hildegard was five years old, she correctly prophesied the color of a calf in the womb.[23] As a young girl, she had yet to understand the meaning of these spiritual gifts, and since they were usually combined with the onset of an illness, she began to think of them as some sort of liability. Liability or not, it is worth mentioning that apart from her spiritual gifts, Hildegard was a sickly child, and she remained in ill health for the rest of her life.

Hildegard's visions, combined with both her extraordinary intelligence as well as her frequent unexplained illnesses, helped her parents in their decision to secure for her the best opportunity to put her talents to use in the service of God. Consequently, Hildegard tells us: "In my eighth year I was offered to God for a spiritual way of life."[24] But like so many of her early years, "when this offering occurred and what it consisted of is open to interpretation."[25] What we do know is that at the age of eight, Hildegard was given as a companion to a pious young woman named Jutta von Sponheim, the daughter of Count Stephan of Sponheim, who was merely six years older than she. Together they lived with Jutta's family in Sponheim, until the two of them were enclosed at the Benedictine monastery in Disibodenberg.[26]

Prior to Hildegard's arrival, when Jutta was just twelve, she became seriously ill. During this time, she vowed to pursue a holy life if only God would heal her, which he did. Thereafter, from about 1106, Jutta embarked on an "unvowed" religious life in the house of Lady Uta, a widow of Göllheim, with eight-year-old Hildegard in tow. After Uta died, Jutta expressed a desire to go on pilgrimage, an idea which was thwarted by her brother, Meinhard, who later became the Count of Sponheim. He headed off his sister's departure by appealing to their acting bishop, Otto of Bamberg (later Saint Otto of Bamberg).

Disibodenberg Enclosure

Bishop Otto persuaded Jutta to do the very opposite of going on a pilgrimage. Instead, he encouraged her to attach herself to a monastery of monks as an *inclusa* or anchoress, "which was a more radical and lasting form of ascetic 'exile' from ordinary life than pilgrimage."[27] This is exactly what she did, bringing Hildegard, who was by then fourteen, and her niece (also named Jutta) with her. It was on All Saints Day, 1112, when "the girls' vows were received by Otto, bishop of Bamberg."[28] Following the formal ceremony, "Hildegard and the two Juttas were literally walled into their living space, with the understanding that they would leave that humble dwelling only upon their death":[29]

> With psalms and spiritual canticles, the three of them
> were enclosed in the name of the most high Trinity. Af-
> ter the assembly had withdrawn, there they were left in
> the hand of the Lord. Except for a rather small window
> through which visitors could speak at certain hours and
> necessary provisions be passed across, all access was
> blocked off, not with wood but with stones solidly ce-
> mented in.[30]

Little is known about these decades of Hildegard's life, except
that her bouts of illness and her visions continued. The elder
Jutta was the only person she told about this, and she, in turn,
informed a monk named Volmar, whose position it was to su-
pervise the nuns and administer the sacraments for them. With
the passing of time, Volmar became Hildegard's "lifelong friend,
confidant, and secretary."[31]

While the idea of becoming an anchoress (recluse), might
seem like quite a leap from going on a pilgrimage (as we know
it), in the twelfth century it wasn't necessarily so, as author and
Hildegard scholar Barbara Newman explains:

> Europe at the turn of the century was aglow with the ar-
> rival of the eremitic life, a cherished ascetic ideal dating
> back to the desert fathers and mothers of the early Chris-
> tian era. In growing numbers, men and women alike
> were forsaking not only marriage but even the security of
> established monasteries to live an austere solitary life as
> free roaming hermits (the preferred option for men) or as
> enclosed recluses (the lifestyle recommended for wom-
> en). Young girls in particular might go to extraordinary
> lengths to adopt such a life, resisting parental demands

with all the determination of martyrs.[32]

When Jutta, her niece, and Hildegard arrived at Disibodenberg, the monastery was a new Benedictine community, which was being built on an ancient religious site. Construction of this monastery began in 1108, and the building campaign, which included a large and impressive church, was finally completed in 1143. Hildegard lived at Disibodenberg longer than anywhere else, with the "noise and bustle of the masons and carpenters"[33] as her constant companions. It was here that she lived, studied, worked, and prayed. Today, the monastery stands in ruins, and ironically enough, it is a pilgrimage site.

In the early part of the twelfth century, it was common to have both a community of monks and a community of nuns living together in a "double monastery." However, Disibodenberg was not like that. In reality, "Jutta's relationship with the community was rather that of a holy woman living within the monastery walls and thus providing luster and the flavor of greater than usual sanctity to the community."[34] As it happened, Jutta turned out to be an "ascetic par excellence."[35] In her book, *Hildegard of Bingen*, Honey Meconi describes Jutta as the stereotypical medieval holy woman and anchoress:

> She wore the "cheapest and meanest of clothing" and both a hair shirt and iron chain, normally right next to her body in order to maximize discomfort. She went barefoot in the winter. She not only went through the psalter daily — and sometimes twice or three times a day — but did this standing or crouching, occasionally prostrating herself after every verse. She ate little, "contenting herself with the left-overs from the common table, though it be a pauper's table, and abstained from meat for eight years."[36]

News of Jutta's piety spread quickly. Some came to see her, while others wrote letters, all asking for her blessing, her counsel, and her prayers. She healed the sick with her laying on of hands and she received divine revelations. But she was no pushover. As a matter of fact, "she struck one uninspired brother dumb and then restored him to health through her prayers."[37]

Where Two or More ...

The combined holiness of Jutta and Hildegard proved to be a magnet for other young women seeking to live a consecrated life. As a result, their small community of women religious grew rapidly as parents approached the Benedictines to accept their daughters, in exchange for gifts (financial and otherwise) to the monastery. "One of those to join the convent was Jutta's well-educated cousin, a young noblewoman named Richardis [von] Stade, who brought with her even more riches and prestige to the community."[38] In time, Richardis became Hildegard's closet friend and companion.

Once Jutta received permission from her superiors, she opened up the stone tomb and "brought inside with her the girls who were to be nurtured under the guidance of her disciplined guardianship."[39] From that point forward, the space that she shared with Hildegard and her niece, Jutta, became a kind of monastery, but in such a way that she was still able to maintain the enclosure, even with the comings and goings of a community. Thereafter, the entrants to the monastery were admitted as nuns, rather than enclosed as anchoresses.

With the growth of the community came a sense of independence. "Rather than being completely dependent upon the monks for food, liturgical services, and religious instruction, with a greater number of recruits more of these activities could be carried out by the nuns themselves."[40] There were also new opportunities for leadership, as well as increased responsibilities. Hildegard, for one, became the administrator for this growing community as well as their recognized spiritual leader and teacher.

She demonstrated the skills to be able to accomplish these tasks, yet Hildegard *always* referred to herself as unlearned, ignorant, and simple. She once referred to herself as a "poor creature formed from a rib."[41] She also tells us that Jutta "was not a scholar."[42] There are those who believe that appealing to her ignorance was just a strategy for Hildegard, and that it was possibly the only approach "for her, as a woman, to be believed when she later made her pronouncements."[43] In other words, in professing her lack of knowledge, Saint Hildegard was confirming that "God, not the unlearned Hildegard, was responsible for what she was saying."[44]

At that time, a formal education was unavailable to women, so neither Jutta nor Hildegard were trained in the seven liberal arts (the trivium of grammar, rhetoric, and logic; and the quadrivium of arithmetic, geometry, astronomy, and music) that formed the curriculum of cathedral and monastery schools. Yet, this does not mean that they were not educated, as both Jutta and Hildegard had learned basic reading literacy before entering the monastery, and they transmitted this to the other women in their formation.[45]

In turn, Jutta taught Hildegard to read the Book of Psalms in Latin and to sing the psalms of the monastic hours, the Divine Office. She also showed her how to play on the ten-string psaltery, a kind of dulcimer plucked by hand. The rest of her education was entrusted to Volmar, her teacher and mentor. Actually, Hildegard's writing suggests "that she was intimately acquainted with an extremely wide range of both older and contemporary writing, and not merely the expected Bible and works by the Church Fathers."[46]

In fact, we have reason to believe that Hildegard was a voracious reader and that the Disibodenberg monastery must have had either a very extensive library or participated in what would have effectively been a really good interlibrary loan system.[47] So for Hildegard, "a lack of human education (*humana doctrina*) was not necessarily a stumbling block, for a major thrust of her prophetic project was to bring the learned philosophers and clerics to their comeuppance. For all their time in the schools, they remained cold and barren."[48]

Jutta's Death

Jutta passed away on December 22, 1136, at the age of forty-five. Together with Hildegard, she had been at Disibodenberg just over twenty-five years. In recent years, the *Life of Jutta* (*Vita Jutta*)[49] has shed new light regarding the timing of her death, which had already been revealed to her in a vision years before. As the story goes:

> Jutta had been forewarned of the timing of her death more than two decades earlier by an old woman called Trutwib, a devout widow who was staying at Disibodenberg on the precise day Jutta (and Hildegard) were to enter anchorage. As Trutwib approached the courtyard of the guesthouse, a vision appeared before her and spoke: "You must know that the lady Jutta who today is to be enclosed in this place, shall happily spend twenty-four years here, and in the twenty-fifth year pass happily from this world. That you may give all credence to my words, you must know that in a short while from today you yourself are to die."[50]

It happened just as predicted, and the old woman died just a few short days later, but not before telling Jutta what she had seen and heard. As the years passed, Jutta began to ponder and prepare for her imminent death.

In the twenty-fourth year, Jutta's strength began to diminish as she engaged in lengthy fasts and vigils in anticipation of her hour. In the early morning hours of December 2, 1136, Jutta saw a vision of a tall, handsome man who introduced himself as Saint Oswald, who was once a king to the English people. He told her in comforting words the exact date of her death. The *Vita Jutta* gives a moving account of her final hours, which appear to have involved her whole community, as well as a few of the monks. To be sure, Jutta denied herself right up to the end:

> After she had been burning in an acute attack of fever for twenty days, she comforted her disciples, ten of them in number, with her soothing counsels. Since she knew the time of her call was drawing near, she asked for *Viaticum*[51] and received it, which she had been accustomed to do almost every day she was lying ill. When she sensed that the hour was almost at hand for her to be led forth from the body, she asked them to read to her the Passion of the Lord. When this was finished, she counselled all who were present to give themselves to the prayers and the psalmody, praying, like her, unceasingly.
>
> In the silent hours of that very night, she surprised everyone there by asking that the holy veil be brought to her quickly. Having placed it on her head, she asked that she be placed on a hair-mat strewn with ashes, earnestly appealing to the bystanders then, as she had before, that they not hinder her by their weeping from moving forward towards her Creator. Thus, placed on her hair-mat in a place convenient for the arrival of the brothers she entreated by a sign that the brothers be called. When they had prayed litanies over her, she then fortified her-

self with the sign of the holy Cross and gave up her holy soul.[52]

Prior to her death, Jutta had begged that she not be "openly uncovered for washing,"[53] so Hildegard and two other women took care of arranging the body. When they undressed her, they discovered a chain "which she had worn on her flesh had made three furrows right around her body, although the body itself shown with a miraculous whiteness."[54] Jutta was first buried in the monastery's chapter house, and later interred before the altar in the Marian chapel. A surprising sadness hung over Hildegard's reaction to Jutta's death, in that she did not react at all.

This leaves us wondering how close they really were, despite their constant companionship of three decades. Regardless, for Jutta, "having died to the world and withdrawn from it, was more fruitful in her one spiritual heir and daughter, Hildegard ... than if she had been given in marriage and brought forth a greater number of offspring through generation of the flesh."[55]

Reflection Questions

Pope Benedict called upon Saint Hildegard to help him clean up the Church. What does this say about the way Catholics interact with the saints?

Which of all of Jutta's personality traits do you find most interesting?

HILDEGARD AS *MAGISTRA*/ ABBESS AND AUTHOR

At age thirty-eight, Hildegard was a natural to succeed Jutta, so it is no surprise that upon her death, the nuns unanimously chose her as their leader. Around this same time, "the archbishop of Mainz ordained a new abbot of Disibodenberg: Cuno, whose name also appears as Cuono and Kuno."[56] The timing of these appointments was about the only thing they had in common, as their relationship was not one of equals. For starters, given the fact that Hildegard's community was subordinate to the male monastery of Saint Disibod, she never carried the official title of "abbess."[57] Instead she was referred to only as *magistra* ("headmistress"). This left Hildegard in the position of being beholden to the abbot of Disibodenberg, a challenge she dealt with for the rest of her life. It was not until the thirteenth century, with the decline of the Disibodenberg community, that Hildegard's successors were able to claim the title of abbess.[58] This is important only for the fact that "except for an occasional queen, abbesses were the most important women in the Middle Ages. ... They had a great deal of spiritual authority and presided over large, complex, and wealthy institutions."[59]

If Hildegard had followed the same ascetic footsteps as Jutta, it is quite possible that we would never have heard of her. But Hildegard was different. She was "not particularly sympathetic to the eremitic life."[60] In contrast to Jutta, Hildegard's attitude was a commonsense notion of balance. She based her entire theology on the harmony of the created world and its relation to God.[61] This is evidenced in the way "she cared for the spiritual and material well-being of her sisters, fostering in a special way community life, culture and the liturgy."[62]

Similarly, Hildegard was not obsessed with suffering just for the sake of suffering. She actually warned against abstaining from eating, "especially when the person concerned is 'fickle and imprudent' or 'preoccupied with immense and serious sufferings, that can cause a variety of pustules, abscesses or tumors, which may have a fatal outcome.'"[63] As a true Benedictine, "she practiced and counselled only moderate fasting and avoided mortification."[64]

Speak and Write of the Wonders ...

The real turning point in the life of Hildegard came not with her election as the *magistra*, but a few years later in 1141. It was then that she experienced a vision unlike anything she had ever experienced before. In the following quote, Hildegard explains this revelation:

> When I was forty-two and seven-months old, Heaven was opened and a fiery light of exceeding brilliance came and permeated my whole brain, and inflamed my whole heart and my whole breast, not like a burning but like a warming flame, as the sun warms anything its rays touch. And immediately I knew the meaning of the exposition of the Scriptures, namely the Psalter, the Gospel and the other Catholic volumes of both the Old and the New Testaments, though I did not have the interpretation of the words of their texts or the division of the syllables or the knowledge of cases or tenses. ... The visions I saw I did not perceive in dreams, or sleep or delirium, or by the eyes of the body, or by the ears of the outer self, or in hidden places, but I received them while awake and seeing with pure mind and the eyes and ears of the inner self, in open places, as God willed it. How this might be is hard for mortal flesh to understand.[65]

It was the most powerful vision yet, not just of lights and images, but of inspiration as well as a complete understanding of "the inner meaning of the texts of her religion."[66] This vision was different in that it was an infusion of knowledge regarding the meaning of Scripture and the content of the Faith in its entirety. It was accompanied by a voice from heaven saying: "O fragile human, ashes of ashes, filth of filth, say and write what you see and hear!"[67] Later, she heard the same instructions: "Speak therefore of the wonders, and being so taught, write them and speak."[68] And another time, she heard a voice from heaven saying: "Cry out therefore, and write this!"[69] Unknown to her at the time, her visions were meant to teach others how to praise God, and "from that praise, to love God's Son, ourselves, and others more, and also to trust the Holy Spirit for healing, forgiveness, and new life."[70]

Feeling unequal to the task, Hildegard fell gravely ill. She interpreted her illness as a sign of God's displeasure, so she finally confided in Volmar about her situation. With his help, and the permission of Abbot Cuno, as well as the support and encouragement of her dearest friend, the nun Richardis, Hildegard began her work on the *Scivias (Know the Ways of the Lord)*, the first of her three major works. With this masterpiece, Hildegard, the fourth woman Doctor of the Church, began a "life of creative production unparalleled among medieval women and men."[71]

A word about Hildegard's illnesses. With all of her great accomplishments, it is hard to believe that she was often so sick that she was unable to get out of bed. Her symptoms suggest that she suffered from severe migraines. There are those who believe that her migraines contributed to Hildegard's ongoing visions, and it is possible that they added to what she saw, but the visions "were too defined, clear, and spiritually rich to be mere symptoms of a malady."[72] In any case, "Hildegard was a master at turning her weaknesses into strengths. Although these migraines and their paralyzing after-effects must have slowed her down some, they never physically impeded her work for long, and she never wavered from her dedication to God's calling."[73]

Scivias (*Know the Ways of the Lord*)
Scivias is not like any of the other classical works by female

saints and mystics. Saint Catherine of Siena's *Dialogue* is an on-going conversation between Catherine and the Father. Saint Te-resa of Ávila's *Interior Castle* teaches the interior path to union with God. And Saint Thérèse of Lisieux's *The Story of a Soul* is an autobiography. Unlike these works, Hildegard's *Scivias* is more of a catechesis than anything else.

It is worth noting that when Hildegard writes about things other than God, her tone is practical and rather matter-of-fact. When she writes about the things of God, however, her language changes completely, involving layer after layer of symbolism and metaphors. It has been said that the "most fascinating part of Hildegard's work is really her 'cosmic theology,' a vision of the universe that is both vast and minute,"[74] which is found in Hilde-gard's major writings. And the good news is that "there is always hope at the end of Hildegard's prophesies."[75]

In *Scivias*, we see that Hildegard was actually more a proph-et than a mystic. She tells the history of salvation by reminding people what God did for them, what he asks of them, and what will happen if they don't obey. In other words, in her "mind's eye," Hildegard grasped the significance of heaven and hell, creation, the Fall, sexuality, and the human person as first and fundamen-tal.

She claimed that the work was necessitated by the failings of the twelfth-century Church. She perceived her time as "an 'ef-feminate age,'"[76] in which the Scriptures were neglected and the Christian people ill-formed."[77] Hildegard believed her task was to do what the bishops and priests of her day had failed to do: proclaim the Gospel, teach the Faith, and remind people that the Day of Judgment was at hand. The fact that she was a woman added insult to injury to these ineffective priests, whose failure had necessitated her mission. She argued that these men had made such a mess of things that "God had to call a weak woman in to save the day."[78]

When they began this project, Hildegard, Volmar, and Richardis worked out a system for recording her visions. First, she would write down what she had seen and heard on wax tablets in her less than perfect Latin. Then Richardis would correct Hildegard's grammar. Finally, Volmar would copy it out neatly onto parchment.[79] The pages of *Scivias* were also illuminated with Hildegard's visions. Most likely, one (or more) of the nuns painted these astonishingly beautiful illuminations under Hildegard's direction.[80]

Hildegard began writing *Scivias* in 1141, and it was a ten-year effort, which is not surprising given her other responsibilities, as well as the size of the book.[81] Here Barbara Newman describes the essence of this work:

> *Scivias* consists of three [books],[82] each made up of a series of visions — six, seven, and thirteen, respectively. In each case, Hildegard first describes her vision and then presents an exegesis delivered, she says, by a "voice from heaven" (formulas such as "And I heard a voice from heaven saying to me ..." mark the passage in the text from vision to explication). Her themes are many: the Trinity, the creation, the fall of Lucifer and the subsequent fall of Adam, the Incarnation, evil and temptation, the Church and its sacraments, the work of the Holy Spirit, wisdom viewed as human knowledge illumined by faith, the steps by which man will be saved, and the Last Judgement. ...
>
> *Scivias* ends with a description of a vast "edifice of salvation" — the City of God — and with a [shorter] version of Hildegard's morality play[83] *Ordo virtutum* (*Play of the Virtues*), which she later set to music and which was intended for performance by her nuns. In the play, the oldest of its kind, the [cast of characters] are allegor-

ical virtues, dwelling within the City of God, who help
a penitent soul to resist temptation and find salvation.
Scivias is, in essence, a book of instruction in how to
best live life so that one may enter the City of God.[84]

During Hildegard's lifetime, *Scivias* was her most celebrated
work. Author and translator Carmen Acevedo Butcher attributes this fame to "the apocalyptic visions of its unforgettable
conclusion. First, the Antichrist rapes the allegorized female *Ecclesia* (the Church). Later the Antichrist is sitting on top of a
mountain of excrement, which signifies sin's disgusting nature,
when a single, divinely sent lightning-bolt knocks this self-ex-
ulting imposter down dead."[85] This is Hildegard. Her visions are
always graphic, bold, and dramatic, but her theology is solid.
Butcher continues:

> While her visions may be stunning, Hildegard's theology
> is always well-grounded. It is in fact literally grounded,
> enough to make the sensitive reader think that perhaps
> Hildegard was also an avid gardener, for her images are
> often of planting and growing. One of the main themes
> of *Scivias* is the fertile virginity of Christ versus the ster-
> ile, unbridled sexual vices of the Antichrist. … Hilde-
> gard shows that all things grow in Christ and are fecund,
> but Satan is [death].[86]

Hildegard was still working on the script when her own insecurity led her to question whether it might be better for her to
stay silent. She hesitated. Who would believe her? Would people
think she was only seeking attention? Would they question her
sanity? Looking for advice, she sought the guidance of the Cistercian[87] monk, Bernard of Clairvaux, who was "one of the most
illustrious preachers and monks from the Middle Ages, and a

figure of immense authority."[88]

Bernard not only encouraged Hildegard to keep writing, but he also interceded on her behalf with Pope Eugenius III,[89] a fellow Cistercian. News of Hildegard's writings had already reached the pope, who at the time was presiding over the Synod[90] of Trier. Given that the German city of Trier was not far from Hildegard's convent in Disibodenberg, Eugenius obtained a copy of her unfinished manuscript, which he read aloud before the assembled bishops. Convinced that Hildegard's text was divinely inspired, "the Pope authorized [Hildegard] to write down her visions and to speak in public."[91] To formalize the matter, he sent her "a letter of apostolic greeting and benediction to continue her work."[92]

It is impossible to overstate the meaning of this seal of approval from the pope. Not only did Eugenius grant Hildegarde his full permission to continue recording her visions, but he also encouraged her to speak in public about the Faith, something unheard of for women at that time. There are those who believe that the medieval Church sought to silence her voice and crush the gifts of this strong and holy woman, but that was not the case. "The pope and those in authority encouraged her labors for God, and Pope Eugenius invited her to preach about them for the good of the faithful."[93]

It is worth highlighting that even though God himself sent her the visions and commanded her to write, Hildegard still sought the endorsement of the Church. In one of his Wednesday audiences, then-Pope Benedict XVI explained why this was so important: "This, dear friends, is the seal of an authentic experience of the Holy Spirit, the source of every charism: the person endowed with supernatural gifts never boasts of them, never flaunts them and, above all, shows complete obedience to the ecclesial authority. Every gift bestowed by the Holy Spirit, is in fact intended for the edification of the Church and the Church, through her Pastors, recognizes its authenticity."[94]

Move to Rupertsberg

By the time she received approval from Pope Eugenius, the word was out that a true prophetess lived on the Rhine. Hildegard's solitude, as limited as it had been, was over. She quickly became a celebrity, and the number of postulants nearly doubled under her leadership. This led to an overcrowding situation at the convent at Saint Disibod. Even as plans to expand the nuns' quarters were underway, Hildegard experienced a new vision, which would have a profound impact on her community. In this vision, Hildegard saw "a place where the river Nahe flows into the Rhine, a hill dedicated in days of old to the name of St. Rupert the Confessor."[95] Rupertsberg, as it was called, is where she believed God was calling her to move the women's community.

It is to be expected that the monks of Disibodenberg were against this move, for they had nothing to gain and everything to lose by the departure of these women. Their monastery had profited handsomely from the presence of both Jutta and Hildegard. Throughout the years, the faithful, "whose visits and request for prayer and intercession would bring gifts — including valuable property — and fame, which led to more gifts and still more fame."[96] Furthermore, during this era, when a woman joined a religious community, she brought a dowry with her. So, from a "purely practical point of view, Hildegard's departure would be disastrous for Disibodenberg."[97] Still, Hildegard persisted. She knew that the nuns should have their own convent, separate from the monastery.

In what seems to be a direct response to the opposition of the monks (as well as some of the nuns and their families), Hildegard once again took to her sick bed, where she lay stone cold without speaking or moving. "She finally triumphed when Abbot Kuno, visiting her bedside, and finding himself unable to lift Hildegard's head or turn her body, became convinced that her illness was a sign of God's displeasure at the delay in the fulfillment of His will, and at last consented to the move."[98] In the end, Hildegard was helped by Archbishop Heinrich of Mainz, who gave his permission and support to help her purchase the Rupertsberg property from its owners. Marchioness von Stade, Richardis' mother, was her main benefactor in this endeavor. At the time, Hildegard had no idea what von Stade had in mind regarding Richardis.

As an interesting aside, before the move to Rupertsberg, Hildegard received a sarcastic letter from another abbess, Mistress Tengswich of the Saint Marien convent near Andernach. She questioned, among other things, Hildegard's reasoning for accepting only wealthy and aristocratic women into her community, which Tengswich believed was un-Christian. Instead of denying it, Hildegard's return letter overlooked the sarcasm and she offered her this rather abstract, but truthful, explanation of the human condition: "Where humility is found, there Christ always prepares a banquet. Thus, when individuals seek after empty honor rather than humility, because they believe that one is preferable to the other, it is necessary that they be assigned to their proper place."[99]

In other words, her belief was "that some lower-born women might join a particular convent, not for spiritual reasons, but as a means of bettering their social standing by associating with the higher nobility. Women of the upper nobility did not gain in worldly honor because of joining a convent, but those of lesser birth may have thought they would gain such honor."[100] For those who have eyes to see, there is wisdom here. In the politically correct world in which we live, saying this would be scandalous, but Hildegard lived during the twelfth century and things were different then.

At last, in 1150, Hildegard moved approximately twenty nuns, all of whom had come from noble families and were used to living in comfort, as well as Volmar, their priest and confessor, from their established quarters at Disibodenberg to the old, decaying, but still standing buildings at Rupertsberg, near Bingen[101] on the Rhine. Even though their financial position was precarious, the nuns had servants and hired workers ready to restore the existing buildings. Still, the task was overwhelming. For some, it proved to be too much, and they simply left. However, they were soon replaced by the daughters of other nobles, who along with their parents were eager to help build this new monastery. With funds from her nuns' families, and other wealthy donors, the restoration began immediately.

Even though the job was immense, Hildegard served as the general contractor. She worked alongside builders, stonemasons, and artists, overseeing every aspect of the project. Rupertsberg included all of the buildings detailed in the Rule of Saint Benedict[102] for self-sufficiency. This included a mill, stables, gardens, and a workshop, as well as a chapel, dormitories, an infirmary, and a cemetery.

It took years to complete, but by 1177, the monk Guibert, Hildegard's last secretary, remarked with awe at all that Hildegard had accomplished, noting that there were now accommodations for fifty nuns:

> Besides this, there is another marvel to consider here: that though this monastery was founded recently — a short space of time ago, that is twenty seven years ago — not by any of the emperors or bishops or the powerful or the rich of any region, but by a woman who was poor, a stranger, and sick; yet it has made such progress in its religious character and in its resources that it is skillfully laid out, not with grand but with commodious dignified buildings most suitable for a religious community, with running water distributed through all the workshops. Furthermore, not counting guests whom we are never

without, and the administrators of the house of which
they have several, the monastery provides enough for
the expenses and clothing of fifty sisters without any
shortfall.[103]

Rupertsberg was not the last of Hildegard's monasteries. In 1165,
she founded another, the convent in Eibingen on the other side
of the Rhine, for women of more moderate means. She was a
frequent visitor, but she never lived there. Named the Abbey of
Saint Hildegard, it was dissolved in 1804, but was restored with
new buildings in 1904, and it exists still to this day.

The Struggle for Richardis

In the midst of all of the restoration projects, Hildegard was
constantly beset by personal and vocational problems. The first
and worst of these problems was the loss of her dearest friend,
Richardis. To her great surprise and disappointment, Richardis'
mother and Hildegard's benefactor, Marchioness von Stade,
had secured another appointment for Ricardis. She secured
this appointment with the help of Richardis' brother, Hartwig,
the Archbishop of Bremen. Richardis was to be the Abbess of
Bassum, a famous monastery to the north. Richardis' niece,
Adelheid,[104] another integral member of the community, was
also offered the opportunity to become an abbess of another
monastery, something that was officially denied Hildegard because of the relationship of her community with the monks of
Saint Disibod.

Whether or not Hildegard saw this as an affront, one thing
was clear: She feared for the health and well-being of both Richardis and Adelheid, and she was determined to prevent their appointments. First, she wrote a letter to Marchioness von Stade,
appealing to her motherly heart, saying:

For this position of abbess that you desire for them is
certainly, certainly, certainly not God's will, nor com-
patible with the salvation of their souls. Therefore, if
you are the mother of these your daughters, beware
not to become the ruin of their souls, for, afterward, although you would not wish it, you would grieve with
bitter groans and tears.[105]

When this approach failed, she appealed directly to the archbishop and then to the pope, but in all cases, she failed to stop
the transfer. By the time of her last appeal, both Richardis and
Adelheid had already moved to their new posts.

Once Richardis was installed as Abbess of Bassum, Hildegard wrote her a heart-wrenching letter, which was her final ac-
ceptance of the reality that Richardis wasn't coming back. For
Hildegard, losing Richardis was a terrible setback. She had been
by Hildegard's side from the time she had arrived at Disibodenberg as a young girl. She had worked closely with Volmar and
Hildegard, assisting with the writing of Hildegard's visions and
the running of the monastery. Hildegard had leaned on Richardis through all of her frequent illnesses, trials, and struggles
with the monks. In this letter, Hildegard confessed to loving her
too much, saying:

Daughter, listen to me, your mother, speaking to you
in the spirit: my grief flies up to heaven. My sorrow is
destroying the great confidence and consolation that I
once had in mankind. From now on I will say: "It is good
to trust in the Lord, rather than to trust in princes" [Ps
117:9]. The point of this Scripture is that a person ought
to look to the living height, with vision unobstructed by
earthly love and feeble faith, which the airy humor of
earth renders transient and short-lived. Thus, a person

looking at God directs his sight to the sin like an eagle. And for this reason, one should not depend on a person of high birth, for such a one inevitably withers like a flower. This was the very transgression I myself committed because of my love for a certain noble individual.

Now I say to you: As often as I have sinned in this way, God revealed that sin to me, either through some sort of difficulty or some kind of grief, just as He has now done regarding you, as you well know. ...

I so loved the nobility of your character, your wisdom, your chastity, your spirit, and indeed every aspect of your life. ... But all the same, may the angel of God go before you, may the Son of God protect you, and may his mother watch over you. Be mindful of your poor desolate mother, Hildegard, so that your happiness may not fade.[106]

It was merely two years before the twenty-eight-year-old [107] Richardis died of a sudden illness, just as Hildegard had predicted. The year was 1152. It was her brother (the Archbishop of Bremen) who broke the news to Hildegard. It appears that he hoped to soften the blow by telling her how much Richardis missed her life at Rupertsberg, saying:

I write to inform you that our sister — my sister in body, but yours in spirit — has gone the way of the flesh, little esteeming that honor I bestowed on her. ... I am happy to report that she made her last confession in a saintly and pious way and that after her confession she was anointed with consecrated oil. Moreover, filled with her usual Christian spirit, she tearfully expressed her longing for your cloister with her whole heart.[108]

Because this was exactly what Hildegard feared would happen, she could have responded to this sad news in any number of ways. However, she rose above it, proving that she was worthy of her suffering. In her brief response, instead of pointing out the error of his ways, she tried to comfort the archbishop with her own memory of Richardis:

> God favored her so greatly that worldly desire had no power to embrace her. For she always fought against it, even though she was like a flower in her beauty and loveliness in the symphony of this world. … Therefore, although the world loved her physical beauty and her worldly wisdom while she was still alive, my soul has the greatest confidence in her salvation. For God loved her more. Therefore, He was unwilling to give His beloved to a heartless lover, that is, to the world.
>
> Now you, dear Hartwig, you who sit as Christ's representative, fulfill the desire of your sister's soul, as obedience demands. And just as she always had your interests at heart, so you now take thought for her soul, and do good works as she wished. Now, as for me, I cast out of my heart that grief you caused me in the matter of this my daughter. May God grant you, through the prayers of the saints, the dew of His grace and reward in the world to come.[109]

As if this wasn't enough, in 1153 both Pope Eugenius and Saint Bernard died, as did her patron, Archbishop Heinrich of Mainz.

Life after Richardis

It took eight long years before the separation from Disibodenberg was complete. During this time, Hildegard was in a constant struggle to increase the sisters' independence from the Saint Dis-

ibod monks. Naturally, this took a toll on her health, which continued to go up and down, depending on the success or failure
of her efforts. "Only in 1158 did she reach an agreement with the
Archbishop Arnold of Mainz (Heinrich's successor), wherein he
granted Hildegard's convent his protection and agreed to regulate the spiritual relations and the distribution of assets between
the Rupertsberg and Saint Disibod communities."[110]

This increased financial independence was accompanied
by other new and unusual expressions of autonomy. For example, Hildegard's nuns developed their own distinctive manner of
dressing:

> They wore long, white, silk veils and golden crowns
> with crosses on both sides and the back, with a figure
> of the Lamb on the front. This held special meaning for
> them, for whom the crown they received in this world
> presaged the celestial reward granted to virgin brides of
> Christ in the next. ... The image of the Lamb signified
> that they followed him wherever he goes, likening the
> nuns at Rupertsburg to the virgins called to the Heav
> enly Jerusalem.[111]

This was another concern raised in the letter by the abbess,
Mistress Tengswich.[112] She took issue with their flowing hair,
white veils, jewels, and crowns, claiming that they violated the
dress code recommended in the Rule of Saint Benedict. "Hildegard's response to Tengswich shows that in the hierarchy of
Hildegard's mind, virgins were the apex of creation. Marriage
was not 'bad,' but Hildegard taught that it was the consequence
of the Fall and therefore could never be a calling as exalted as
virginity."[113] As she saw it, her nuns were virgins, and virgins
symbolized Eve before the Fall, standing in the "unsullied purity of paradise, lovely and unwithering."[114] The white of their

garment and veil, therefore, reflected this, as did their flowing hair and the small circlet upon their heads.[115]

Reflection Questions
What was the lesson that Hildegard learned from the Richardis situation?

What did you think of Hildegard's responses to Mistress Tengswich's complaints?

HILDEGARD'S CREATIVITY

In addition to building her first new monastery, caring for her nuns, mourning the loss of Richardis, and a whole host of other things, Hildegard also spent the 1150s through the 1160s pouring herself and all of her creative energy into her new home, her work, her writings, and her music. It was almost as if she were "born again." Her enthusiasm for artistic matters is particularly endearing. We might say that the activities of the 1150s finally established her persona. After spending years in the enclosure of Disibodenberg, she was finally free to fully express herself.

Ordo virtutum (The Play of the Virtues)
Just two years after Hildegard and her nuns made the move to Rupertsberg, construction had advanced enough that Hildegard thought it was time for a celebration. So she invited the aristocratic families of the Rupertsberg nuns, the Archbishop of Mainz, and the monks from Disibodenberg to join her for the May 1, 1152 dedication of the newly renovated chapel. To mark the occasion, she expanded her *Ordo virtutum (The Play of the Virtues)*, which was first featured at the end of *Scivias*. This symbolic drama is "a splendid staging of the Soul's struggle with the

Devil. It is also the earliest surviving morality play, and the only one whose author is known."[116]

In four scenes, *The Play of the Virtues* tells the tale of the soul's fall and redemption. However, it doesn't just tell the tale; it sings it. In this way, the play is like a mini opera, with most of the dialogue sung. There is only one character in the play who doesn't sing — the Devil. Instead of singing, he shouts his lines, signifying that he has "divorced himself from all heavenly harmony."[117] By all accounts, Hildegard reserved the role of the Devil for Volmar, probably as a joke on him. The other nineteen characters — a chorus of Old Testament prophets, the Soul, and the Virtues — sing the words written by Hildegard to music that she herself composed. The monks most likely played the patriarchs and prophets, and Hildegard's nuns sang the remaining roles of the Soul and the Virtues. Knowledge of God, Humility, Chastity, Respect for the Awe-Inspiring God, Contempt for the World, Obedience, Faith, Hope, and Charity are just a sampling of the Virtues. In the play, each one explains how it helps the Soul to grow and mature in grace.

In her book *Hildegard of Bingen: A Spiritual Reader*, Carmen Acevedo Butcher summarizes the spirit of this morality play:

> Hildegard's *Play of the Virtues* has a simple dynamic structure. The prologue presents a chorus of law-abiding Old Testament patriarchs and prophets, rightly astonished to see the numinous New Testament Virtues. When the Devil enters in scene one, he starts seducing the Soul. This temptation is swiftly executed, and the fallen Soul exits, her sinning taking place discreetly offstage during scene two. Hildegard crafted this prudent staging with the high-born religious sensibilities of her audience in mind.
>
> In scene two, each Virtue explains who she is and

what she contributes to the fight for the Soul's health. The Devil interrupts this chorus of Virtues to mock them. In scene three, the bedraggled Soul reappears, obviously traumatized but repentant. She converses with the Virtues, and the Devil is silent. In scene four, the Devil makes one last attempt to ensnare the Soul, but she resists, the Virtues tie the Devil up, and they all praise God for the victory.

The final section presents mystical words from Jesus on the cross, sung as the Virtues walk triumphantly through the church, with the forgiven Soul marching at the back of the procession, in the place of honor.[118]

Liber vitae meritorum (The Book of Life's Merits)

In 1158, six years after the performance of *The Play of the Virtues*, Hildegard was at it again, this time picking up the theme of the virtues once more in a book entitled *Liber vitae meritorum* (*The Book of Life's Merits*). Completed five years later, in 1163, it is a "study of the human weaknesses that separate us from God."[119] This book "focuses on our moral flaws, seemingly inherent in human consciousness, and the role of repentance and the virtues in re-establishing our union with God."[120]

It details a series of six visions where embodied versions of vice and virtue converse with one another, with each making the case for why humans should embrace one over the other. Again, Carmen Acevedo Butcher summarizes Hildegard's work:

This book's six visions focus on the temptations every Christian encounters and how God can help those who love Him resist these. Hildegard details thirty-five vices, plus their punishments and fitting acts of penance. Traditionally, the vices were presented as all-female (partly because the Latin nouns for these abstract concepts are feminine), but Hildegard presents the sins mostly as hideous creatures that are a mix of human and beast. In doing so, she made sin as ugly as possible and also avoided denigrating women.

In *The Book of Life's Merits*, joy is praised as the earthly reward for obeying God. Hildegard also shows that the spiritual rebels who choose not to follow God experience a worldly sadness that can neither see nor participate in the ubiquitous divine happiness. The disobedient are seen as literally dry and lifeless.[121]

Physica (Natural History) and Causae et curae (Causes and Cures)

In her determination to help care for the many sick and afflicted who came to the monastery for assistance, and in an effort to stay true to the Benedictine tradition of giving aid and comforting the sick, Hildegard studied natural sciences and medicine. Because she was gifted with remarkable powers of observation, she cataloged their illnesses, their treatment, and their cures, as well as the qualities of all the herbs and medications. According to author Fiona Maddocks, this was not all that surprising:

> The Middle Ages was a time of taxonomy. Europe was beset with a desire to classify, to make lists of things and group them in the world, and to order them like an index of the book of Creation. Bestiaries[122] and herbals, cosmographic diagrams and maps had started appearing during the previous century. ...
>
> Advances in agriculture prompted numerous studies of husbandry. Animals, birds, fish, trees, stones, plants, and stars all had to be listed and described, not only for the quixotic pleasure of their existence, but also

for their medicinal or spiritual purpose. This was not empirical science but the necessary gathering of data which precedes it. Hildegard was as assiduous as any in her desire to catalogue, to comprehend, to control.[123]

Her books *Physica* (*Natural History*) and *Causae et curae* (*Causes and Cures*), both written in the 1150s, arose out of this desire for knowledge. When it came to the subject matter detailed in *Physica* (a study of plants, animals, stones, minerals, and metals) and in *Causes and Cures* (a medical handbook), Hildegard never claimed divine inspiration or infused knowledge. She doesn't explain how she came by such detailed knowledge, but it is likely that she learned it from the monks at Disibodenberg, perhaps working alongside them in their infirmary or receiving personal instruction from them, so that the growing community of women could have a doctor of their own within their cloister.

For her time, Hildegard was not out of the mainstream in terms of her scientific and medical knowledge. Rather, her work reflected the standard beliefs of that age. These beliefs were based on what is called the four "humors" and the system of medicine organized around them, which influenced European medicine from the time of the Roman Empire until at least the 1700s. This system held that there were four bodily fluids: blood, phlegm, black bile, and yellow bile. In a healthy person, these four bodily fluids should be in balance. However, most people were seen as having a mild excess of one of the humors, which determined not only their temperament but also their propensity to sickness and the kinds of disorders they could be expected to have.

Physica is divided into nine books, and the way Hildegard approached this subject gives us a clear example of her well-ordered personality. In her book *Hildegard of Bingen*, scholar Honey Meconi unpacks Hildegard's strategy, telling us:

Each [of the nine] books cover one component of the
natural world, in the order [of] plants, elements, trees,
stones, fish, birds, animals, reptiles, and metals. Discussions of each item, for which Middle High German
names are given, do not include physical descriptions
but rather whether it is hot or cold, wet or dry. If it has
medicinal or healthful value, instructions as to how to
prepare and use it are included. Some of these are un-
likely to have much practical utility, such as the directive "If one has the ague [malaria-like symptoms] take
a mouse and give it a blow so that it cannot run away.
Before it dies, tie the back of the mouse between the
shoulder blades. ... Let the mouse die between the person's shoulder blades, and that person will be cured."[124]

Building upon what she had already written, Hildegard's *Causes
and Cures* is both a cosmological text and a medical handbook
woven together from a variety of complex ideas. The first section
of the book is devoted to an account of man and his relationship
with the cosmos and the world of created things. The second
section places man within this context, and having explained a
version of the humoral theory, begins to introduce a series of
illnesses and disorders that afflict human beings. Next, she provides information on medieval pharmacology and herbal healing. The final section is a mixed bag, where Hildegard discusses
the differences between male and female, gynecology, human
sexuality, embryology, sleep and dreams, signs predicting death
or survival, and astrological influences. What ties it all together,
however, is not so much her medical expertise, but rather,

the concern for taking care of the sick person more than
the sickness; an attention given to behaviors as effects of
some inner disorder; beauty and harmony as necessary

for human development — all principles that are necessary to Hildegard's thought. For her, the natural state
of a human is health, the lack thereof is destructive. Re-
trieving, maintaining, protecting a person's natural health,
assuring the full use of his or her capabilities, in the business of daily vigilance over both spirit and body.[125]

Liber divinorum operum (The Book of Divine Works)

Hildegard's third major work, *The Book of Divine Works*, was
the result of a vision of such force that Hildegard described it as
mysterious and wonderful, causing her whole body to convulse
to the point that she lost all bodily sensation. Hildegard wrote of
the voice that commanded her to describe the visions, as well as
her reaction, saying:

> Give others an accurate account of what you see with
> your inner eye and what you hear with your soul's inner
> ear. Your testimony will benefit others. As a result, men
> and women will learn how to get to know their Creator,
> and they will no longer refuse to adore God with excel-
> lence and respect.
>
> That voice made me — heartbroken and fragile
> creature that I am — begin to write with trembling hand,
> even though I was traumatized by more illnesses than I
> could count. As I started this task, I looked to the true
> and Living Light and asked, 'What should I write down?'
> I was never in a condition similar to sleep, nor was I in
> a spiritual ecstasy. I saw the vision with the inner eye of
> my spirit and grasped them with my inner ear.[126]

She started this work in 1163 and completed it in 1173, by then
an old woman of seventy-five. *The Book of Divine Works*[127] is
divided into three unequal parts, with a total of ten visions. The

genesis of the work is rooted in her meditations on the Prologue to the *Gospel of John*. Professor Nathaniel Campbell, who in 2018, finalized the first complete English translation of this work, claims that the visions are "the most complex of Hildegard's corpus, each revealing different aspects of the Work of God (*opus Dei*), i.e. both humankind and all creation unfolding and acting across salvation history."[128] Campbell continues:

> Each vision of the work elaborates the dynamic Word of God, present before and then within Creation, becoming a human being to bring the Work of God — humanity and by extension all creation — to perfection. This grand vision is the culmination of Hildegard's entire theological project and represents her most mature formulation of themes intrinsic to her thought.
>
> These include the fundamental human vocation to understand both ourselves and all creation as the work of God, and our place as cooperative agents of that work; such rational understanding as the means to come to know our Creator and properly fulfill the work for which we were created; the relationship between humanity and the rest of creation as microcosm and macrocosm; and the eternal predestination of the incarnate Word of God irrupting and unfolding through time as revealed both in Scripture and the life of the Church.
>
> The scope of Hildegard's visionary theology is both cosmic and close — reflections of God's loving self-revelation are both grand and utterly intimate, as the Work of God reaches from the very heart of infinity down into every smallest detail of the created world.[129]

Quite unexpectedly, in 1173, while Hildegard was putting the final touches on *The Book of Divine Works*, Volmar died. For almost sixty years, Volmar had been Hildegard's teacher, confessor, friend and secretary, in addition to serving as provost for the convent at Rupertsberg. He had edited all her books and letters, advised her through her troubles with abbots and kings, and encouraged her in all her work. Her grief was matched only by the death of Richardis twenty years earlier. Hildegard and Volmar had grown old together, and with his death, she had now lost the two people she had loved the most. Given that he was younger than the elderly (and chronically ill) Hildegard, Volmar had dreaded the day when Hildegard would finally return to her Lord,[130] yet he never lived to see it.

The *Vita*

Apart from her sorrow, Hildegard needed another secretary. She had no choice but to turn, once again, to the monks at Disibodenberg, who still had authority over her in appointing priests. This was unfortunate because the tension between Hildegard and the monks still existed. As a matter of fact, then-Abbot Helenger refused to replace Volmar until he was forced into it by a delegate of Pope Alexander III. Only then did he send the monk Gottfried to serve as provost and secretary to Hildegard and her fifty nuns. Providentially, it was Gottfried who, in late 1174 or early 1175, started work on the *Vita Sanctae Hildegardis* (*The Life of Saint Hildegard*), and from this project comes much of what we know about Hildegard today. This new arrangement was short-lived, however, as Gottfried died in 1176, leaving the *Vita* unfinished.

Shortly before Gottfried died, Hildegard had begun corresponding with a French-speaking monk named Guibert of Gembloux. In 1177, he traveled from Flanders (now Belgium) to Rupertsberg. Like Gottfried before him, Guibert became the provost for the monastery and also Hildegard's secretary. He served in this capacity for the last three years of Hildegard's life, during which time he added to the *Vita*, but did not finish it. Several years after her death, her friends commissioned another monk, Theoderic of Echternach, to complete the project. In her essay "Sibyl of the Rhine: Hildegard's Life and Times," Barbara Newman tells the backstory of how Theoderic concluded the *Vita*:

> Theoderic was apparently chosen more for his literary reputation than his personal interest in the saint; he seems to have had no direct acquaintance with Hildegard and little knowledge of her works. So instead of resuming the narrative where Gottfried had left off, Theoderic made an extraordinary choice: He decided to fill book 2 of the *Vita* with memoirs that Hildegard herself had dictated to help her earlier biographer, interspersing his own awed if sometimes uncomprehending comments. Thus, the *Vita* permits us to compare three diverse perspectives on Hildegard's life: her own, the perceptions of a monk who worked for her, and the imagination of a far more distant admirer.[131]

Aside from the *Vita*, Hildegard's own literary output was immense. Beyond her three mystical works and her individual books on medicine and the natural sciences, she penned nearly four hundred letters (most of which still exist) to people of all walks of life from all over Europe, including four popes, emperors, bishops, secular rulers, monks, and nuns. Some of this correspondence shows her involvement with the titanic events of her era. For instance, there is communication between King Henry II of England and his queen, Eleanor of Aquitaine, and a letter of encouragement to Saint Thomas Becket before his martyrdom. These documents are truly the gateway to Hildegard's soul, in that they reveal not only the extent of her popularity, but also her own ways of seeing herself. In the words of Pope Benedict, "They bear witness to the attention Hildegard paid to the events of her time, which she interpreted in the light of the mystery of God."[132]

She also wrote fifty-eight teaching homilies that were addressed directly to her nuns and fellow monastic leaders. Added to that were several biographies, including separate biographies for both Saint Disibod and Saint Rupert, as well as several minor works. This twelfth-century cloistered nun even invented her own language ("Unknown Language"), which was a "collection of invented and whimsical words organized by themes. The words, mostly nouns, are a combination of German and Latin."[133] Accompanying this was her own alternative alphabet. There was simply no limit to Hildegard's work and creativity.

Hildegard's Music

While the majority of Catholics are just getting acquainted with Hildegard, the world of music has spent the last forty years honoring her as one of the world's earliest known named composers (most medieval composers are anonymous). Her popularity comes in spite of the fact that there are no mentions of her music in any reference book before 1979, and she barely warranted an entry in the 1990 edition of the popular *The New Grove Dictionary of Music*. Even so, celebrations of "Hildegard the composer" began in 1979, when the British musician Philip Pickett and his New London Consort decided to commemorate the 800th anniversary of Hildegard's death by singing four of her original compositions in concert.

Much of the world — musical and non-musical — had never heard of her work, but her unique style, which makes fairly radical departures from the plainchant typical of the twelfth century, sparked a desire to rediscover Hildegard's music and writings. Biographer Fiona Maddocks puts Hildegard's newfound fame in context:

The surprise Hildegard breakthrough, as it might be

called, came in 1983 when *A Feather on the Breath of God* — the title borrowed from *Scivias* — won a coveted *Gramophone* award. The collection of sequences and hymns, edited and directed by Christopher Page and sung by members of Gothic Voices, unexpectedly made the classical best seller charts and spawned a batch of further recordings by other groups.[134]

Christopher Page spent a great deal of time researching and editing Hildegard's music for *A Feather on the Breath of God*, and he admits that there is some mystery regarding the composition of this piece:

> We don't know if Hildegard is sitting and humming the songs, or if she's perhaps humming and writing them down on a white tablet, with a final version then being written by someone else on slate or parchment. We don't know if the words come first, or if the words and the music grow together in an organic development. We don't know how much hand in it her male helpers — male secretaries and priests — had. None of that is clear.[135]

Whatever the case, Hildegard "always maintained that her musical gift, like her visions and her understanding of Scripture came to her without any human instruction: She recorded the songs and taught them to her nuns just as she had heard them by celestial voices."[136]

Like most things in Hildegard's life, she began writing music because the circumstances demanded it. Hildegard's *Vita* concurs with this, explaining that she began composing music for her nuns to sing the Divine Office shortly after becoming prioress of the women's community at Disibodenberg. A form of Gregorian chant, Hildegard's music has a free-flowing rhythm, and much of it has wider leaps and is bolder and more exciting than other composers' music written in her time. Her "compositions" stand out from other liturgical music because of the almost spontaneous nature of her melodies: They are freer, more wide-ranging and elaborate than the simple, one-octave lines advocated by her mentor, Bernard of Clairvaux. Hildegard's choice of hymn subject was diverse, ranging from the Creator, Son, and Holy Spirit, to the saints, and most especially, to the Blessed Virgin Mary.

Although a few historians doubt that Hildegard even wrote the compositions that bear her name, most credit her with composing an expansive collection of liturgical music (known as *Symphonie armonie celestium revelationun* or The Symphony of the Harmony of Celestial Revelations), in addition to the music that accompanied her *Play of the Virtues*. Today, a total of seventy-seven of her songs have survived the centuries, the largest amount of music to come down to us from a single medieval composer. It is important to remember, however, that "during her lifetime, and until very recently, it was not Hildegard's music that led to her fame; rather it was her spirituality. ... Her music can only be understood as one facet of a creativity that mirrored and was generated by her religious beliefs." [137]

Hildegard's music and her three theological works, together with copies of her letters, her *Vita*, and her "Unknown Language," have all been preserved in a manuscript called the *Riesencodex*, which weighs over thirty pounds. Only her medical and scientific works (*Physica* and *Causae et curae*), were not included in this manuscript. Despite nearly being destroyed during World War II, the *Riesencodex* still exists and is kept in the Hochschul und Landesbibliothek RheinMain (formerly the Hessische Landesbibliothek or State Library of Hesse). [138] Today it is fully digitized.

Reflection Questions

Hildegard was not necessarily known for her medical expertise. Rather, she was known for her concern for taking care of the sick more than the sickness. She paid attention to certain behaviors, particularly the effects of some inner disorder, with beauty and harmony as necessary for human development. For her, the natural state of a human is health, the lack thereof is destructive. How does this compare to the way we practice medicine today?

If you could choose to play one of the virtues in Hildegard's *Play of the Virtues*, which one would it be? Would it be Knowledge of God, Humility, Chastity, Respect for the Awe-Inspiring God, Contempt for the World, Obedience, Faith, Hope, Charity, or another virtue of your choice? Remember that it will be your job to explain how this virtue helps the soul to grow and mature in grace.

PUBLIC LIFE

With the early encouragement of Pope Eugenius, Hildegard lived a very public life. It is rare, and in fact practically unheard of, for a contemplative nun to leave the convent without abandoning her vocation. A Benedictine vocation, in particular, requires stability, a key element of the commitment made by the nun when she makes her final vows.[139] But this did not deter Hildegard. By the time she began speaking publicly about the affairs of the Church, she was sixty years old and already famous, which may have helped her overcome, or simply ignore, any obstacles. Regardless, when Hildegard spoke, people listened.

Between 1158 and 1171, Hildegard made four very public and highly publicized speaking tours around Germany. During those thirteen years, she visited twenty-four cities and preached in every cathedral that would have her, and she was welcomed everywhere she went. Even the prelates she attacked so vehemently invited her to preach in their churches. Called "Sibyl of the Rhine"[140] by her contemporaries, Hildegard was a sensation wherever she preached. Laity and clerics alike packed the cathedrals to hear her rail against the corruption in the Church and prophesize about the end times. She was always firm in calling priests to be faithful, to turn away from abuses, and to focus on teaching the message of Jesus Christ. Author and professor Dr. Brennan Pursell gives us some insight into Hildegard's state of mind in his article "St. Hildegard of Bingen: A Visionary for All Time":

> She held nothing back when lacerating corrupt clergymen and prelates for their abuses of the Church, of selling offices and allowing themselves lives of pomp, luxury, and plentiful sexual pleasures. When a prior wrote to her to ask her to pray for him because he was doing so for her and wanted a good outcome for his affairs, she scolded him roundly for his selfishness and pagan understanding of prayer.[141]

While it is true that much of Hildegard's preaching was directed toward the corrupt clergy, she also used this same energy against the curse of the Cathars,[142] a heretical group[143] storming through Europe at that time, becoming more powerful by the day. As a matter of fact, "by 1165, the Cathars were so numerous and so strongly supported by many of the nobles that they were preaching their heresy openly,"[144] while the bishops stood back in fear of taking action against them.

Among other things, the Cathars had a twisted understanding of good and evil. They denied the omnipotence of God and instead asserted the existence of two gods: the evil god of the

204 *Saint Hildegard of Bingen*

Old Testament and the good god of the New Testament. According to the Cathars, the evil god created the world and all that it contains, including the human body, while the good god created all things spiritual, including the human soul. In this dualistic worldview, all matter was evil, and the goal of human existence was to escape the body and dwell forever in the spiritual realm of the good god. In other words, body: bad; soul: good. If souls weren't pure enough at the time of death, or if they retained any attachment to the material world, they would be incarnated (and continue to be reincarnated) until they achieved true spiritual maturity.

Although the Cathars borrowed some of the Catholic Church's hierarchical offices, calling their leaders priests and bishops, they rejected almost everything else about the Church, especially the Incarnation, Christ's saving death, and all of the sacraments, save for their own version of confession (called *Consolamentum*). As the Cathars saw it, a good God would never take on matter; Christ's suffering in the body could secure nothing good for humanity; and God could never impart his life to men through material things — through bread, wine, water, oil, or the laying on of hands. In addition, "they denounced marriage, forbade sexual intercourse and held that suicide was both lawful and commendable."[145] For those who could not curb their sexual drives, the Cathars encouraged homosexuality or even bestiality, so that no children would be born. These extremist views left few options open to the survival of the human race.

Despite all of this, the Cathars prevailed because of their deceitful appearance of "holiness." People left the Church in droves to follow them because they were looking for something outside the Church, which they saw as becoming ever more corrupt. The faithful were impressed by the Cathars' austere way of life, which sharply contrasted with the greed and ostentation of many of the local prelates and clergy. The grievous lack of preaching and teaching of orthodox doctrine only added to the problem. This specific issue was at the heart of Hildegard's frustrations, and it was with a heavy heart that she wrote in the *Scivias*: "The Catholic Faith wavers among the people and the Gospel goes limping among them, and the powerful volumes that the learned doctors explicated with great study ebb away in shameful apathy, and the food of life of the divine Scriptures has been allowed to grow stale."[146]

In an effort to counteract this scandal, the Church tried diplomacy and polite excommunications, but these yielded little fruit. Then, at the urging of his bishop, Saint Dominic Guzman founded the Order of Preachers (often called the Dominicans), whose austere lifestyle and orthodox sermons, as well as the flexibility to travel wherever error was taught, were intended to counteract the Cathars' witness. Dominic hoped that an order of holy priests, who truly lived and taught the Faith, could show the people that the Church, not the Cathars, possessed the fullness of the truth. Saint Dominic and his band of Dominicans did make significant inroads in some places, but the Cathars still remained strong.

Beginning in 1209, Pope Innocent III ordered a crusade known as the Albigensian Crusade (or the Cathars Crusade), to reduce the Cathars' numbers. The geographical scope of the Crusade stretched across southern France. Atrocities were committed on both sides, and the papal legates representing the interests of Pope Innocent III were often led more by their passionate hatred of the Cathars than by the pope's wishes. As they saw it, the Cathars posed a threat to the whole human race. The Albigensian Crusade officially came to an end with the Treaty of Paris in 1229. The Cathars, however, still remained, which led the Church to begin a formal Inquisition to root out their remaining members. By the end of the thirteenth century, long after Hildegard's death, the Cathars had all but died out.

Hildegard's battle with the Cathars was sadly not her last battle. The last year of her life proved to be more painful and disruptive than any since her troubled move to Rupertsberg three decades earlier. In 1179, Hildegard got caught up in an exceedingly bitter battle with the prelates of the archbishopric of Mainz. In that year she had allowed the body of a certain nobleman (name unknown) to be buried in the consecrated grounds of Mount Saint Rupert. At some point earlier in his life, this gentleman had been excommunicated. While Hildegard acknowledged this, she argued (correctly) that he had been fully reconciled with the Church before he died.

Despite Hildegard's protestations, and without the approval of the archbishop, who was in Rome at the time, the prelates demanded that she exhume the body and remove it from the sacred grounds. Hildegard refused, on the basis that it would be a grievous sin to do so. She also made sure the grave was well hidden to ensure that the body would not be taken without her knowledge. There are even reports that "Hildegard lifted her staff over the grave, and, making the sign of the cross, she caused it to disappear."[147]

As a result, Hildegard and her nuns were, for a time, prohibited from hearing Mass, receiving the Eucharist, and from singing the Divine Office, which they were simply to recite. "The penalty deprived the abbess of music for the first time since her childhood, and during the long silence of the choir, she reflected on the meaning of music, its charismatic nature, and its place in the divine scheme of things."[148] She claimed that "to silence music in Church is to create an artificial rift between heaven and earth, to put asunder what God has joined together."[149] For Hildegard, music is quintessentially human. "Mankind was never meant to live without it."[150] Finally, after many months of going back and forth, with Hildegard calling on her friends in the Church hierarchy, the interdict was lifted in March 1179, six months before her passing on September 17, 1179.

We know nothing of her final months other than that Hildegard "had grown weary of 'this present life,' especially given her recent battles and struggles."[151] She knew that her journey was coming to an end because God had told her, and she repeatedly told her daughters that it would happen very soon. The account of Hildegard's death found in the *Vita* reads as follows:

> And thus the blessed virgin had labored in a serious illness for some time, when in the eighty-second year of her life, on the fifteenth day before the Kalends of October [17 September], she was freed from the toilsome prison of this life and went with a happy passage to her heavenly spouse, whom she had longed for with her whole heart. Her daughters, to whom after God, she had been all joy and all solace, wept bitterly as they took part in the funeral rites of their mother.
>
> For though they did not doubt her reward and the favours that would be conferred on them by God through her, yet they were afflicted with the most intense grief of heart over her departure, by which they seemed to lose the unique consolation of her through whom God had visited them. But God clearly showed even in her passing through a manifest miracle how great was the standing she had before him.[152]

Reflection Questions

During times of trouble for the Church, God always raises up someone. He raised up Dominic, Teresa, Catherine, Thérèse, and Hildegard. Who is he raising up now?

Hildegard believed that silencing music in church creates an artificial rift between heaven and earth. How did this affect our worship during the COVID-19 pandemic, when most dioceses and parishes were not allowing congregational singing as a measure to prevent the spread of the virus?

HILDEGARD'S LEGACY

It has been said that Hildegard was a "remarkable woman in an age of remarkable men."[153] Yes, that is true, but Hildegard was and is so much more. She loved God above all and sacrificed everything to please him. She has motivated countless numbers of people even up until our own day. She endured enormous sufferings. She fought the good fight and persevered to the end. Quite simply, she is a great saint.

Still, in the post-Christian world in which we live, Hildegard is not without controversy. Some people claim that she was a narcissistic fraud, or at the very least, just plain crazy. Many Catholics are concerned that Hildegard may not be a reliable source, as she has become something of an icon for people with interest in the New Age, and for radical feminists. Indeed, it seems that today Hildegard has become all things to all people. For example, "New Age reformers invoke her name over crystals and feminists see her as their mother."[154] On this point, Professor Brennan Pursell highlights how the New Age movement has adopted Hildegard for all the wrong reasons:

> [Hildegard] is not an unknown quantity in Germany today, but most people know her name for the wrong reason. There is a product line and a .com[155] named after her that hawk herbal elixirs, potions, creams, powders, rocks, and ointments, all marketed to improve one's general happiness and feeling of freedom and independence. … The products claim to be based

on her writings, but they are more in line with new-age commercialism. More serious and more worthy is the association (*Bund der Freunde Hildegards*) that publishes a quarterly journal and includes a network of doctors, chiropractors, and medical researchers who make a real effort to apply her remedies and methodologies to problems people face today.[156]

Unfortunately, this group has missed Hildegard's religious message almost entirely. Her teachings were meant to help people gain sanctification and salvation. And while it is true that Hildegard's writings are sprinkled with a feminist bent, the meaning of the word "feminist" has evolved over the centuries, and it is certain that she would have rejected the rhetoric of the modern women's liberation movement.

Hildegard was discovered in the English-speaking world just as gender and women's study programs were becoming serious academic disciplines. Consequently, there is an ever-increasing interest in her in the universities. "For these new disciplines the rediscovery of the life and works of Hildegard of Bingen can be compared to what the discovery of the Dead Sea Scrolls meant for biblical scholars."[157] Hildegard's many accomplishments and especially her writings (translated into English for the first time), are perfect fodder for these growing disciplines.

By declaring her a Doctor of the Church, Pope Benedict XVI recaptured Hildegard for "authentic Catholicism and genuine mysticism rooted in the perfection of the virtues and a love for Jesus Christ."[158] In light of the many crises facing the Church, it is easy to see the hand of God in Hildegard's return from the past. Like Teresa, Catherine, and Thérèse, Hildegard lived a life of hope. She not only survived, but she thrived during her remarkably long life. For Hildegard, hope opened up new horizons, making her capable of dreaming of what wasn't even imaginable.[159] The hope within her inspired to go forth with faith and to answer every time God called. More importantly, her hope helped other people to hope, as she was a tremendous inspiration to others, even up to the pontificate of Pope Benedict XVI.

Saint Hildegard of Bingen, pray for us!

Reflection Questions

What about Hildegard's life do you find the most interesting?

Hildegard was deeply rooted in the Christian virtue of hope. Think of an example in her life when this was especially true.

Conclusion

"Hope is the same thing as remembering."[1] I love that quote, and it seems very appropriate for the conclusion of this book. When I began this project, I admitted to being very disheartened and embarrassed about the ongoing scandals in the Catholic Church. I felt that I was losing hope in the Church I love so much.

In the course of writing this book about the four women Doctors of the Church, I have asked myself over and over again, *What is hope?* Better yet, *What is Christian hope?* I quickly learned that hope is not a whimsical virtue. It is not the same as optimism. For example, hoping for a sunny day is not actually hope, at least in the Christian understanding of the word. True hope is rooted in eternity; it is always looking forward. While true hope does not deny "the reality of the pain and suffering in the world, it looks beyond the present grief to the reality of the Resurrection."[2] In essence, hope is living each day for tomorrow. You might even say that hope "draws the future into the present."[3] Most importantly, learning to hope comes from prayer, for God is the source of all hope.

No one knew this better than Teresa of Ávila, the Doctor of Prayer. Early in her life, Teresa of Ávila came to understand that life is a journey, taken one step at a time. We now know that young Teresa had no deep desire to join the convent. It was only after weighing her options that she was able to move forward in answering what she knew to be God's call, against her father's wishes. Unsure of the future, she proceeded in hope. Once she joined the convent, however, she never stopped moving, and this is a true sign of hope. By placing her hope and trust in the Lord, Teresa founded convents all over Spain — seventeen for women and fifteen for men. She also left Catholics of all walks of life a blueprint on how to pray, which has been and still is a gift to millions of people who are searching for God. During the course of her sixty-seven years, Teresa experienced every hardship on earth. Still, she never gave up, hoping and trusting always that God would be there for her. He did not disappoint.

Catherine also learned hope at a very young age. He came early in her life, as she was only six years old when she saw her first vision, which became both a prophetic image of her future mission, and a betrothal to her beloved spouse. Of all the difficult things God asked of Catherine and all of the trials that she had to endure, perhaps the most daunting was when he asked Catherine to help bring the papacy back to Rome from Avignon, France. An arduous task, no doubt, but Catherine had hope and persevered despite numerous setbacks. Eventually, the papacy did return to Rome, if only for a while. Despite the many challenges and sufferings facing the Church in her day, Catherine never stopped hoping and praying that the Church would be healed.

Thérèse is a saint of a different sort, and she learned hope in very different ways. Losing her mother at the age of four was her defining moment, and everything stemmed from there. Her greatest hope and desire was to follow her older sisters into the Carmelite convent. So great was her hope that she even petitioned the pope to allow her to enter religious life early. Throughout her life, Thérèse embodied the "pilgrim nature of the Christian life, which is a life moving toward something not yet fulfilled."[4] Thérèse knew that she was not made for this life. In fact, everything Thérèse suffered in this life was made possible because of her longing for the eternal. The most special thing about Thérèse is that she gives *us* hope. She promised that she would spend her heaven doing good on earth, and anyone who has ever appealed to her knows this is true.

In Hildegard, we find a woman whose life combines aspects of the three other women Doctors. Hildegard spent over twenty years as a contemplative nun, until God called her to a more active life when she was thirty-eight years old. It is reasonable to think that in those thirty-eight years, God was silently preparing Hildegard for an adventure like no other. How else do you explain this amazing, holy woman of God? Hildegard, founder of two new religious communities, visionary and mystic, teacher and preacher, author, musician and doctor, was most of all an expert in humanity. Even to the very end, when her music was taken from her, she never grew bitter, and she never lost hope.

There is a German proverb, "Hope is the last to die."[5] However, Pope Emeritus Benedict XVI, a German, rejects this notion, saying: "No, hope never dies. It is literally built in view of eternity and has its foundation in eternity. All that is earthly passes away, but hope in Jesus is confidence in a life that truly begins only in a new dimension."[6]

In closing, I ask myself once again, what is hope? There is no doubt that all four of these brilliant women, these Doctors of the Church, would certainly agree that hope "is you and me walking together, humbly bearing Christ's brilliant light to a world weary of darkness."[7]

Notes

INTRODUCTION

1. Pope Francis, *On Hope* (Chicago, IL: Loyola, 2017). Kindle Edition.

PART ONE: SAINT TERESA OF ÁVILA

1. Angela Blardony Ureta, AO Carm, "Rediscovering Teresa of Ávila: A Lay Perspective," The Order of Carmelites, n.d., accessed December 22, 2020, http://ocarm.org/en/content/ocarm/rediscovering-teresa-avila-lay-perspective.

2. Shirley de Boulay, *Teresa of Ávila: An Extraordinary Life* (New York: Blue-Bridge, 2004), 1.

3. Pope Benedict XVI, *Spe Salvi*, accessed December 21, 2020, Vatican.va.

4. Elizabeth Ruth Obbard, *La Madre: The Life and Spirituality of Teresa of Ávila* (United Kingdom: St. Pauls, 1994), 10. Obbard does not indicate the original citation.

5. Teresa of Ávila, *The Book of Her Life*, in *The Collected Works of St. Teresa of Ávila*, Volume One, Otilio Rodriguez, OCD, and Kieran Kavanaugh, OCD, trans. (Washington, D.C.: ICS Publications, 1987), I, 1, 54. (Hereafter, cited as

Life.) Unless indicated otherwise, in citing Teresa's works, following the title, the first Roman numeral will indicate the chapter, and the second number will indicate the paragraph or numbering given in the translation of her works by Kavanaugh and Rodriguez. Following this is the page number.

6. Ibid., I, 4, 55.

7. Ibid., I, 3, 55.

8. Ibid., I, 7, 56.

9. The Introduction is written by Otilio Rodriguez, OCD, and Kieran Kavanaugh, OCD, translators of *The Book of Her Life*, in *The Collected Works of St. Teresa of Ávila*, Volume One.

10. *Life*, "Introduction," 16.

11. *Life*, II, 7, 60.

12. du Boulay, *Teresa of Ávila: An Extraordinary Life*, 10–11.

13. *Life*, II, 8, 60.

14. Ibid., III, 1, 61.

15. Ibid., III, 5, 63.

16. Ibid., IV, 1, 64.

17. Ibid., IV, 1, 64.

18. Ibid, V, 2, 70.

19. In religious life, a postulant (sometimes called a pre-novice) is someone who is preparing to be admitted into a religious community. It is the first stage of religious life before becoming a novice. Instead of following the strict Carmelite Rule where all are treated the same, the Carmelite Convent of the Incarnation had a "class system," in which the women of means were given fewer menial tasks than those with a lesser standing.

20. Obbard, *La Madre, The Life and Spirituality of Teresa of Ávila*, 31.

21. See *Life*, V, 8, 74.

22. *Life*, V, 9, 75 and VI, 1, 76.

23. Ibid., VI, 2, 77.

24. See ibid., VI, 6, 79.

25. See du Boulay, *Teresa of Ávila: An Extraordinary Life*, 23.

26. Peter Thomas Rorhbach, *Conversation with Christ: The Teaching of St. Teresa of Ávila about Personal* Prayer (London: Aeterna Press, 2016), Kindle Edi-

tion. The original was released by TAN Books in 1980.

27. *Life*, IV, 7, 66–67. Teresa's copy of Osuna's book is still preserved in the sacristy of the first convent she founded, Saint Joseph's in Ávila.

28. See ibid., IX, 1, 100.

29. Ibid., VII, 1, 82.

30. Ibid., VII, 16, 90.

31. Ibid., VII, 14, 89.

32. See Father Christopher Rengers, OFM Cap, and Matthew Bunson, *The 35 Doctors of the Church*, Revised Edition (Charlotte, NC: TAN Books, 2014), Kindle Edition.

33. See *Life*, VII, 16, 90.

34. This is actually a small statue of the bloody face of Christ, only about a foot tall. It is still venerated at the monastery of the Incarnation in Ávila.

35. *Life*, IX, 1, 100–101.

36. Ibid., IX, 3, 101.

37. Teresa of Ávila, *The Interior Castle*, in *The Collected Works of St. Teresa of Ávila*, Volume Two, Otilio Rodriguez, OCD, and Kieran Kavanaugh, OCD, trans. (Washington, D.C.: ICS Publications, 1980), V, 2, Kindle Edition (hereafter cited as IC). First Roman numeral stands for the dwelling place, second number is the chapter.

38. *Life*, IX, 8, 103.

39. See *Life*, XXVIII, 1, 237.

40. *Life*, XXVIX, 4, 247.

41. This extraordinary account was the inspiration of Bernini's dramatic sculpture of Saint Teresa in the famous Church of Santa Maria della Vittoria in Rome.

42. See Rengers and Bunson, *The 35 Doctors of the Church*.

43. Tomás Álvarez, OCD, and Fernando Domingo, OCD, *The Divine Adventure: St. Teresa of Ávila's Journeys and Foundations* (Washington, DC: ICS Publications, 2015), 12.

44. Saint Teresa's nuns still follow the primitive rule of Saint Albert, which is carefully balanced between solitude, work, and common life. They live and pray together, but keep silence for most of the day, including meals. In the evening, they meet for an hour for relaxation and conversation.

45. See William T. Walsh, *St. Teresa of Ávila* (Charlotte, NC: TAN Books, 1987), 175.

46. Rengers and Bunson, *The 35 Doctors of the Church.*

47. Obbard, *La Madre, The Life and Spirituality of Teresa of Ávila*, 55.

48. Teresa of Ávila, *The Way of Perfection Study Edition*, Otilio Rodriguez, OCD and Kieran Kavanaugh, OCD, trans. (Washington, DC: ICS Publications, 2000), 4, 7, Kindle Edition.

49. Tomas Alvarez, *St. Teresa of Ávila: 100 Themes on her Life and Work*, trans. Kieran Kavanaugh, OCD (Washington, D.C: ICS Publications, 2011), Kindle Edition.

50. Obbard, *La Madre, The Life and Spirituality of Teresa of Ávila*, 56.

51. Ibid.

52. *Life*, XXXIII, 2, 285.

53. Ibid., XXXII, 14, 282.

54. Obbard, *La Madre, The Life and Spirituality of Teresa of Ávila*, 59–60, quoting from Allison Peers translation of *The Book of her Life*. See *Life*, XXXIV, 3.

55. See *Life*, XXXIV, 3, 294.

56. Teresa of Ávila, *Spiritual Testimonies* in *The Collected Works of St. Teresa of Ávila*, Volume One, Otilio Rodriguez, OCD, and Kieran Kavanaugh, OCD, trans. (Washington, D.C.: ICS Publications, 1987), 3, 1, 382.

57. Walsh, *St. Teresa of Ávila*, 217.

58. Ibid., 225.

59. Du Boulay, *Teresa of Ávila: An Extraordinary Life*, 102.

60. See ibid.

61. Du Boulay, *Teresa of Ávila: An Extraordinary Life*, 102.

62. Ibid.

63. Ibid.

64. Ibid.

65. Walsh, *St. Teresa of Ávila*, 246.

66. Du Boulay, *Teresa of Ávila: An Extraordinary Life*, 102.

67. See ibid.

68. Abbé Rodolphe Hoornaert, *Saint Teresa in Her Writings* (New York: Benzinger Brothers, 1931), 229.

69. According to Kieran Kavanaugh, OCD, translator of Teresa's writings, this story has been verbally passed down through the centuries, but it is not located in any of her writings. It is part of the oral tradition attached to Teresa of Ávila.

70. Rengers and Bunson, *The 35 Doctors of the Church*.

71. *Life*, IV, 9, 68.

72. Ibid., VIII, 5, 96.

73. Rengers and Bunson, *The 35 Doctors of the Church*.

74. Father Hugh Kelly, SJ, *Saint Teresa of Ávila* (Dublin, Ireland: Irish Messenger Office, 1945), 14. See also The Traveller, "Saint Teresa of Ávila, by Father Hugh Kelly, SJ," CatholicSaints.info, accessed December 22, 2020, http://catholicsaints .info/saint-teresa-of-avila-by-father-hugh-kelly-sj/

75. Ibid.

76. Abbé Rodolphe Hoornaert, *Saint Teresa in Her Writings*, 228.

77. Teresa of Ávila, *The Interior Castle*, in *The Collected Works of St. Teresa of Ávila* (Study Edition), Vol. Two, Otilio Rodriguez, OCD, and Kieran Kavanaugh, OCD, trans. (Washington, D.C.: ICS Publications, 1980), Prologue, 27.

78. Abbé Rodolphe Hoornaert, *Saint Teresa in Her Writings*, 253.

79. See Teresa of Ávila, *The Collected Letters of Teresa of Ávila*, Kieran Kavanaugh, OCD, trans. (Washington, DC: ICS Publications, 2001), Kindle Edition. (Tomás Alvarez has located 468 letters.)

80. IHS: a monogram of the name of Jesus Christ. See newadvent.org, "IHS".

81. See Du Boulay, *Teresa of Ávila: An Extraordinary Life*, 119.

82. See Foley, *The Book of Her Foundations: A Study Guide*, Kindle Edition.

83. Du Boulay, *Teresa of Ávila: An Extraordinary Life*, 120.

84. Ibid.

85. See ibid.

86. Obbard, *La Madre*, 81.

87. Du Boulay, *Teresa of Ávila: An Extraordinary Life*, 121.

88. See Raymond G. Helmick SJ, "Teresa of Ávila," Help Fellowship, Inc., accessed December 22, 2020, http://www.helpfellowship.org/Articles%20of%20 Interest/teresa_of_avila_by_raymond_helmick_SJ.htm.

89. Reverend Hugh Kelly, SJ, *Saint Teresa of Ávila*, 3. The text of this book is taken from the pamphlet "Saint Teresa of Ávila" by Father Hugh Kelley, SJ, 3rd

edition, SQPN. See https://www.scribd.com/document/38138379/Saint-Teresa-of-Avila-by-Father-Hugh-Kelly-SJ.

90. Obbard, *La Madre*, 149.

PART TWO: SAINT CATHERINE OF SIENA

1. See Mary O'Driscoll, OP, *Catherine of Siena: Passion for the Truth — Compassion for Humanity* (New York: New City Press, 2010), 7.

2. O'Driscoll, OP, *Catherine of Siena: Passion for the Truth — Compassion for Humanity*, 7.

3. See ibid.

4. Bull of Pope Pius II for the Canonization of Saint Catherine of Siena, June 19, 1461.

5. Homily of the Pope Paul VI, St. Peter's Basilica, October 4, 1970, Catherine of Siena, Doctor of the Church. Reprinted from *L'Osservatore Romano*, English edition, October 15, 1970, 6–7.

6. Blessed Raymond of Capua, OP (1330–1399), was a leading member of the Dominican Order and served as its Master General from 1380 until his death in 1399.

7. Blessed Raymond of Capua, *The Life of Saint Catherine of Siena* (Rockford, IL: TAN Books, 2003), 54.

8. The Hundred Years' War (1337–1453) involved a long series of conflicts between England and France over the control of the French throne. Just when it looked as if England was finally the conqueror, a young Saint Joan of Arc (1412–1431) appeared on the scene, and she was instrumental in rescuing France. In many ways, the lives of Saint Joan and Saint Catherine mirror one another.

9. The Black Plague (aka the Black Death) arrived in Europe by sea in October 1347. Over the next five years, it killed twenty million people in Europe — almost one-third of the continent's population.

10. Giovanni Boccaccio, *The Decameron*, trans. Mark Musa and Peter Bondanella (New York: Signet Classics, 2002), 10.

11. Raymond of Capua, *The Life of Saint Catherine of Siena*, 25.

12. Ibid., 26.

13. Ibid., 41–42.

14. See ibid., 46.

15. Ibid., 43.

16. Edmund G. Gardner, *The Road to Siena: The Essential Biography of St. Catherine* (Brewster, MA: Paraclete Press, 2009), 24.

17. See Raymond of Capua, *The Life of Saint Catherine of Siena*, 44.

18. Ibid., 47.

19. Ibid., 62.

20. Gardner, *The Road to Siena: The Essential Biography of St. Catherine*, 24.

21. Raymond of Capua, *The Life of Saint Catherine of Siena*, 71, 78.

22. Ibid., 79.

23. Ibid.

24. O'Driscoll, *Catherine of Siena: Passion for the Truth — Compassion for Humanity*, 14–15.

25. Raymond of Capua, *The Life of St. Catherine of Siena*, 107.

26. See O'Driscoll, *Passion for the Truth: Compassion for Humanity*, 9.

27. Raymond of Capua, *The Life of St. Catherine of Siena*, 108.

28. O'Driscoll, *Passion for the Truth: Compassion for Humanity*, 9.

29. Ibid.

30. Gardner, *The Road to Siena*, 39.

31. H.C. Graef, *The Way of the Mystics* (Cork, Ireland: The Mercier Press, Ltd. Corp., 1942), 28. This book is out of print, but it can be accessed at http://www.drawnbylove.com/Graef%20article.pdf (accessed December 22, 2020).

32. See Catherine of Siena, *The Dialogue*, trans. Suzanne Noffke, OP (New York: Paulist Press, 1980), Introduction, 8.

33. While it is true that on a natural level, Catherine could neither read nor write, tradition has it that at one point in her life, Jesus himself taught Catherine these skills.

34. Gardner, *The Road to Siena*, 4.

35. Raymond of Capua, *Life of St. Catherine of Siena*, 304.

36. Ibid.

37. See O'Driscoll, *Catherine of Siena: Passion for the Truth — Compassion for Humanity*, 10.

38. Catherine M. Meade, CSJ, *My Nature is Fire: Saint Catherine of Siena* (New

York: Alba House, 1991), 35.

39. Pope Boniface XIII, *Unam Sanctam*, November 18, 1302.

40. The Avignon popes were all legitimately elected. They may have been French, but they were still popes.

41. Petrarch, "On the Papal Court at Avignon," ed. Colman J. Barry, OSB, in *Readings in Church*, Vol. 1, accessed December 22, 2020, http://archive.org /stream/readingsinchurch009633mbp/readingsinchurch009633mbp_djvu.txt, 470.

42. Don Brophy, *Catherine of Siena: A Passionate Life* (BlueBridge Publishing: New York, 2010), 147.

43. See Gardner, *The Road to Siena*, 53.

44. Brophy, *Catherine of Siena: A Passionate Life*, 148.

45. Ibid., 150.

46. Ibid, 151–152.

47. Raymond of Capua, *Life of St. Catherine of Siena*, 303.

48. See O'Driscoll, *Catherine of Siena: Passion for the Truth — Compassion for Humanity*, 10.

49. Raymond of Capua, *Life of St. Catherine of Siena*, 305.

50. Saint Catherine of Siena, *Letters of Catherine Benincasa* (Glasgow, Scotland: Good Press Publishing, 2019), Kindle Edition.

51. Saint Catherine of Siena, *Letters of Catherine*, Kindle Edition.

52. Ibid.

53. Ibid.

54. Paul Murray, OP, *In the Grip of Light: The Dark and Bright Journey of Christian Contemplation* (New York: Bloomsbury, 2012), 89.

55. Catherine of Siena, *The Letters of St. Catherine of Siena* (Tempe, AZ: Arizona Center for Medieval and Renaissance Studies, 2001), #45, Vol. II, 286–287.

56. Murray, *In the Grip of Light: The Dark and Bright Journey of Christian Contemplation*, 90.

57. Ibid., 90–91, quoting Francesco Malavolti, *Fontes vitae s. Catharinae Senensis: il processo Castellano*, Vol. X, ed. M.H. Laurent (Milan, 1942), 377.

58. Giuliana Cavallini, OP, *Catherine of Siena* (New York: Geoffrey Chapman, 1998), 3.

59. Catherine of Siena, *The Dialogue*, trans. Suzanne Noffke, OP (New York: Paulist Press, 1980), #23, 60.

60. Ibid., #19, 57.

61. Ibid., #116, 216.

62. Ibid., #148, 311–312.

63. Brophy, *Catherine of Siena: A Passionate Life*, 225.

64. Ibid., 219.

65. Catherine of Siena, *The Letters of Catherine of Siena*, ed. Suzanne Noffke, #T373, 364–370.

66. It is a well-accepted fact that, during her life, Catherine ate very little, mostly subsisting on the Eucharist and water.

67. Thomas McDermott, OP, "Catherine of Siena and Leaving the Church," *Catholic World Report*, April 27, 2012, accessed December 22, 2020, https://www.catholicworldreport.com/2012/04/27/catherine-of-siena-and-leaving-the-church/.

PART THREE: SAINT THÉRÈSE OF LISIEUX

1. Patrick Ahern, *Maurice & Thérèse: The Story of Love* (New York: Doubleday, 1998), 11.

2. Ibid.

3. Ibid.

4. Father Fred Miller recorded reflection, "St. Thérèse of Lisieux — 'Jesus, Make Me Resemble You,'" October 1, 2016, accessed December 22, 2020, https://www.youtube.com/watch?v=jtxX4n5--i8.

5. Patrick Ahern, *Maurice & Thérèse: The Story of Love*, 5–6.

6. Peter-Thomas Rohrbach, OCD, *The Search for Saint Thérèse: A Study of the Life, The Legend, The Mystery of Saint Thérèse* (New York: Hanover House, 1961), 16.

7. Ibid.

8. Ibid.

9. Ibid.

10. Ibid.

11. Apostolic Letter of his Holiness Pope John Paul II, *Divini Amoris Scientia*,

October 19, 1997, accessed December 22, 2020, Vatican.va.

12. Right Reverend Monsignor Vernon Johnson, "St. Teresa of Lisieux," EWTN, accessed December 22, 2020, https://www.ewtn.com/catholicism/library/st-teresa-of-lisieux-5619.

13. Peter-Thomas Rohrbach, OCD, *A Study of the Life, The Legend, The Mystery of Saint Thérèse*, 12.

14. The Basilica of Notre-Dame d'Alençon is a Gothic parish church located in Alençon, France. It was elevated to the rank of minor basilica by Pope Benedict XVI in 2009.

15. Father Stéphane Joseph Piat, OFM, *A Family of Saints: The Martins of Lisieux: Saints Thérèse, Louis, and Zélie* (San Francisco: Ignatius Press, 2016), Kindle Edition.

16. Blessed Zélie and Louis Martin, *A Call to a Deeper Love: The Family Correspondence of the Parents of St. Thérèse of the Child Jesus, 1863–1885,* trans. Ann Connors Hess, ed. Francis Renda (New York: Society of St. Paul, 2011), 60–61. (Hereafter cited as CD.)

17. Frederick L. Miller, STD, *The Trial of Faith of Thérèse of Lisieux* (New York: St. Pauls, 1998), 1.

18. Piat, *A Family of Saints: The Martins of Lisieux: Saints Thérèse, Louis, and Zélie*, Kindle Edition.

19. Ibid.

20. CD, 105.

21. Ibid., 106.

22. Ibid., 109.

23. Marc Foley, OCD, *The Context of Holiness: Psychological and Spiritual Reflections on the Life of St. Thérèse of Lisieux* (Washington, D.C.: ICS Publications, 2008), 6.

24. Saint Thérèse of Lisieux, *General Correspondence, Volume I, 1877–1890,* trans. John Clarke, OCD (Washington, D.C.: Institute of Carmelite Studies, 1982), 557. (Hereafter cited as GC I.)

25. Guy Gaucher, *The Story of a Life: St. Thérèse of Lisieux* (San Francisco: HarperCollins Publishers, 1987), 18.

26. See ibid.

27. Saint Thérèse of Lisieux, *Story of a Soul*, trans. John Clarke, OCD (Washington, D.C: ICS Publications, 2005), 22 (hereafter cited as SS), quoting a letter from Zélie to Pauline dated May 14, 1876.

28. Ibid., 18.

29. Ibid., 27. This would play out later in her life when applied to choosing all of the sacrifices.

30. Gaucher, *The Story of a Life: St. Thérèse of Lisieux*, 18.

31. Joseph F. Schmidt, FSC, *Everything is Grace: The Life and Way of Thérèse of Lisieux* (Ijamsville, Maryland: The Word Among Us Press, 2007), 74.

32. Rohrbach, *The Search for Saint Thérèse*.

33. Pope Pius XI, *Miserentissimus Redemptor*, May 8, 1928, accessed December 22, 2020, Vatican.va.

34. Ibid.

35. Rohrbach, *The Search for Saint Thérèse*, 53.

36. Ibid, quoting Pope Pius XII from *The Pope Speaks*, vol.1, no. 3, page 212, 1954. Original in Latin.

37. Schmidt, FSC, *Everything is Grace*, 73.

38. Ida Friederike Gorres, *The Hidden Face: A Study on St. Thérèse of Lisieux*, trans. Richard and Clara Winston (San Francisco: Ignatius Press, 2003), Kindle Edition. Originally written in German in 1959.

39. Ibid.

40. SS, 34.

41. Ibid.

42. Ibid.

43. Schmidt, Everything is Grace, 75.

44. Foley, *The Context of Holiness: Psychological and Spiritual Reflections on the Life of St. Thérèse of Lisieux*, 5.

45. Ibid.

46. SS, Introduction, xvi.

47. Ibid.

48. Ibid., 16.

49. Rohrbach, *The Search for Saint Thérèse*, 56. Original in Latin.

50. SS, 279 (Chronology).

51. Rohrbach, *The Search for Saint Thérèse*, 57.

52. Ibid., 58.

53. Foley, *The Context of Holiness*, 15.

54. SS, 35.

55. Foley, *The Context of Holiness*, 15–16.

56. See ibid., 16.

57. Guy Gaucher, *The Spiritual Journey of St. Thérèse of Lisieux* (London: Darton, Longman & Todd Ltd., 1987), 32.

58. Foley, *The Context of Holiness*, 21.

59. Rohrbach, *The Search for Saint Thérèse*, 75, quoting Pope Pius XI, *Vehementer exultamus hodie*: Bull of Canonization of Saint Thérèse of the Child Jesus and the Holy Face, May 17, 1925, accessed December 22, 2020, http://www.papalencyclicals.net/stt02002.

60. SS, 34–35.

61. See Rohrbach, *The Search for Saint Thérèse*, 72.

62. See ibid., 73.

63. Gorres, *The Hidden Face: A Study on St. Thérèse of Lisieux*, Kindle Edition.

64. Ibid.

65. SS, 58.

66. Ibid.

67. Gaucher, *The Story of a Life: St. Thérèse of Lisieux*, 45.

68. Gorres, *The Hidden Face*, paraphrasing SS, 60.

69. Ibid.

70. SS, 61.

71. He later retracted this. St. Vitus' dance (chorea) is a neurological disorder characterized by rapid, uncoordinated jerking movements primarily affecting the face, hands, and feet. It usually resolves itself within a matter of months without treatment.

72. Gorres, *The Hidden Face*.

73. Rohrbach, *The Search for Saint Thérèse*, 95.

74. Ibid., 96, quoting Marie but no original source noted.

75. SS, 64.

76. Ibid., 65–66.

77. Ibid., 62.

78. Rohrbach, *The Search for Saint Thérèse*, 97.

79. *SS*, 60.

80. Rohrbach, *The Search for Saint Thérèse,* 103. Original in Latin.

81. General Correspondence, trans. John Clarke, OCD, *Letters of St. Thérèse of Lisieux, Volume 1* (Washington D.C: ICS Publications, 1982), 173, footnote 1.

82. See SS, 67.

83. See Marc Foley, OCD, *The Love That Keeps Us Sane: Living the Life of St. Thérèse of Lisieux* (New York: Paulist Press, 2000), Kindle Edition.

84. SS, 77.

85. Ibid., 79.

86. Rohrbach, *The Search for Saint Thérèse,* 106.

87. General Correspondence, trans. John Clarke, OCD, *Letters of St. Thérèse of Lisieux, Volume 1,* 226.

88. SS, 84.

89. Saint Thérèse of Lisieux, *Story of a Soul, (Study Edition),* trans. John Clarke, OCD, prepared by Marc Foley, OCD (Washington, DC: ICS Publications, 2005), Kindle Edition.

90. SS, 53.

91. Ibid., 88.

92. Ibid., 93.

93. Ibid., 97.

94. Ibid.

95. Ibid., 98.

96. Léonie had just returned home from spending seven weeks with the Poor Clares in Alençon. The lifestyle was too difficult for her.

97. Gorres, *The Hidden Face.*

98. SS, 98.

99. Ibid.

100. Rohrbach, 111–112. Rohrbach is quoting Céline, but he does not list an original citation.

101. SS, 98.

102. See Rohrbach, *The Search for Saint Thérèse,* 113.

103. Thérèse was 5'4".

104. SS, 99.

105. Ibid.

106. Gorres, *The Hidden Face*.

107. Ibid. Gorres is paraphrasing this exchange from *SS*, 107.

108. SS, 108.

109. SS, 111.

110. SS, 123.

111. Saint Thérèse of Lisieux, *The Story of a Soul* (Study Edition), trans. John Clarke, OCD, Kindle Edition.

112. Gaucher, *The Spiritual Journey of St. Thérèse of Lisieux*, 73.

113. Gorres, *The Hidden Face*.

114. Saint Thérèse of Lisieux, *The Story of a Soul* (Study Edition).

115. Gorres, *The Hidden Face*.

116. SS, 123.

117. Ibid., 121.

118. Ibid., 122.

119. Ibid., 134.

120. Ibid.

121. Ibid., 135.

122. Ibid.

123. Ibid., 136.

124. Rohrbach, *The Search for Saint Thérèse*, 121.

125. SS, 143.

126. Ibid., 147–148.

127. Ibid., 148.

128. Teresa of Ávila, *The Way of Perfection Study Edition*, Otilio Rodriguez, OCD, and Kieran Kavanaugh, OCD, trans. (Washington, D.C: ICS Publications, 2000), 4, 7. Kindle Edition. Saint Teresa later changed the number of nuns from thirteen to twenty-one.

129. SS, 149.

130. Ibid.

131. Gaucher, *The Story of a Life: St. Thérèse of Lisieux*, 93.

132. Saint Thérèse of Lisieux, *The Story of a Soul* (Study Edition).

133. Ibid.

134. Ibid. This is from the "Notes from Manuscript(s)," under Chapter VII.

135. Ibid.

136. Gaucher, *The Story of a Life*, 99.

137. Thérèse had a holy card with this image imprinted on it, with the words, "Jesus, make me resemble you."

138. Rengers and Bunson, *The 35 Doctors of the Church.*

139. SS, 194.

140. Schmidt, *Everything is Grace*, 31.

141. SS, 210.

142. Ibid., 211.

143. *Carmelite Studies: Experiencing St. Thérèse Today*, ed John Sullivan, OCD (Washington, D.C: ICS Publications, 1990), 115.

144. SS, Epilogue, 271.

145. Saint Thérèse of Lisieux, *Her Last Conversations*, trans. John Clarke, OCD (Washington, D.C: ICS Publications, 1977), 126.

146. Miller, *The Trial of Faith of Thérèse of Lisieux*, viii.

147. SS, Epilogue, 263.

148. John Beevers, *Storm of Glory: The Story of St. Thérèse of Lisieux* (New York: Image Books, 1955), inside front cover.

149. Right Reverend Monsignor Vernon Johnson, "St. Teresa of Lisieux."

PART FOUR: SAINT HILDEGARD OF BINGEN

1. D. D. Emmons, "St. Hildegard of Bingen: A woman ahead of her time," *Our Sunday Visitor*, April 24, 2018, accessed December 22, 2020, https://osvnews .com/2019/04/24/st-hildegard-of-bingen-a-woman-ahead-of-her-time/. There does not seem to be a compelling reason, other than the fact that her cause languished, people died, and life went on.

2. See Rengers and Bunson, *The 35 Doctors of the Church*, chapter 21.

3. Barbara Newman, "St. Hildegard, Doctor of the Church, and the Fate of Feminist Theology" in *SPIRITUS: A Journal of Christian Spirituality* 13(1): Spring 2013.

4. Ibid.

5. Ibid. It should be noted that Hildegard never fell out of favor in the academic circles in Germany.

6. Nathaniel M. Campbell, "The prophetess and the pope: St. Hildegard of Bingen, Pope Benedict XVI, and prophetic visions of church reform," *Postmedieval: A Journal of Medieval Cultural Studies* 10.1, 22–3, 5

7. Ibid.

8. Pope Benedict XVI, "Address of His Holiness Benedict XVI on the Occasion of Christmas Greetings to the Roman Curia," December 20, 2010, accessed December 22, 2020, Vatican.va.

9. Campbell, "The prophetess and the pope: St. Hildegard of Bingen, Pope Benedict XVI, and prophetic visions of church reform."

10. Rengers and Bunson, *The 35 Doctors of the Church*.

11. Fiona Maddocks, *Hildegard of Bingen: The Women of Her Age* (London: Faber and Faber, Ltd., 2013), Kindle Edition.

12. The Rhine River is divided into four sections: High Rhine, Upper Rhine, Middle Rhine, and Lower Rhine.

13. Heinrich Schipperges, *The World of Hildegard of Bingen: Her Life, Times, and Visions*, trans. by John Cumming (Collegeville, MN, 1998), 12.

14. See Paul Senz, "Catholic Composers: Hildegard von Bingen" in *The Catholic World Report*, September 17, 2019, accessed December 22, 2020, https://www.catholicworldreport.com/2019/09/17/catholic-composers-hildegard-von-bingen/.

15. Maddocks, *Hildegard of Bingen: The Women of Her Age*.

16. Ibid.

17. The timeline for the Renaissance is generally thought of as the time between the fourteenth and seventeenth centuries.

18. Mary T. Malone, *Four Women Doctors of the Church: Hildegard of Bingen, Catherine of Siena, Teresa of Ávila, Thérèse of Lisieux* (Maryknoll, NY: Orbis Books, 2017), Chapter 1, Kindle Edition. Also, Pope Benedict XVI: "It is possible to speak of two different theological models: 'monastic theology' and 'scholastic theology.' The representatives of monastic theology were monks, usually abbots, endowed with wisdom and evangelical zeal, dedicated essentially to inspiring

and nourishing God's loving design. The representatives of Scholastic theology were cultured men, passionate about research; they were magistri anxious to show the reasonableness and soundness of the Mysteries of God and of man, believed with faith, but also by reason." Pope Benedict XVI, "General Audience: 28 October 2009," http://www.vatican.va/content/benedict-xvi/en/audiences/2009/documents/hf_ben-xvi_aud_20091028.html.

19. See ibid.

20. See Leroy Huizenga, "Hildegard of Bingen: Sybil of the Rhine, Singing Still," *First Things*, September 16, 2011.

21. Maddocks, *Hildegard of Bingen: The Women of Her Age.*

22. See *Jutta and Hildegard: The Biographical Sources*, trans. Anna Silvas (University Park, PA: The Pennsylvania State University Press, 1998), 158.

23. See ibid., 267.

24. Ibid., 158.

25. Honey Meconi, *Hildegard of Bingen (Women Composers)* (Urbana, IL: University of Illinois Press, 2018), Kindle Edition.

26. Named after Saint Disibod.

27. See *Jutta and Hildegard: The Biographical Sources*, trans. Silvas, 53.

28. Barbara Newman, "'Sybil of the Rhine': Hildegard's Life and Times" in *Voice of the Living Light: Hildegard of Bingen and Her World*, ed. Barbara Newman (Los Angeles: University of California Press, 1998), 5.

29. Meconi, *Hildegard of Bingen.*

30. See *Jutta and Hildegard: The Biographical Sources*, trans. Silvas, 53.

31. Barbara Newman, *Sister of Wisdom: St. Hildegard's Theology of the Feminine* (Los Angeles: University of California Press, 1987), Kindle Edition.

32. Newman, "'Sybil of the Rhine,'" 5.

33. Ibid., 6.

34. Meconi, *Hildegard of Bingen.*

35. Newman, ed., *Voice of the Living Light: Hildegard of Bingen and Her World*, 6.

36. Meconi, *Hildegard of Bingen*, quoting *Jutta and Hildegard: The Biographical Sources.*

37. Ibid.

38. Carol Reed-Jones, *Hildegard of Bingen: Woman of Vision* (Bellingham, WA: Paper Crane Press, 2004), 10.

39. Meconi, *Hildegard of Bingen*.

40. Sabina Flanagan, *Hildegard of Bingen: A Visionary Life*, second edition (New York: Routledge, 1998), 36.

41. Joseph L. Baird, *The Personal Correspondence of Hildegard of Bingen* (New York: Oxford University Press, 2006), Kindle Edition, Letter #3.

42. *Jutta and Hildegard: The Biographical Sources*, trans. Silvas, 160.

43. Meconi, *Hildegard of Bingen*.

44. Ibid.

45. Campbell, "Re: Hildegard's schooling," email message to Terry Polakovic, September 4, 2019.

46. Meconi, *Hildegard of Bingen*.

47. Campbell, "Re: Hildegard's schooling."

48. Nathaniel M. Campbell, "The Authorship and Function of the Chapter Summaries to Hildegard of Bingen's *Liber divinorum operum*," Union College, Barbourville, Kentucky.

49. The *Life of Mistress Jutta, the anchoress* [Hereafter *Vita Jutta*]. The biography of Hildegard's teacher and abbess, Jutta of Sponheim, has only recently surfaced as an essential source and is still being assessed. It throws new light on Hildegard's childhood that does not always match other sources concerning her early years. It is thought to have been written around the time of Jutta's death (1136), perhaps by the monk Volmar, who appears to have been secretary to both women. *Vita Jutta* is the first half of the book *Jutta and Hildegard: The Biographical Sources*, which combines the individual stories of Jutta and Hildegard.

50. *Jutta and Hildegard: The Biographical Sources*, trans. Silvas, 77.

51. Holy Communion given to the dying to assist them on their journey.

52. Ibid., 79.

53. Ibid., 80.

54. Meconi, *Hildegard of Bingen*.

55. Silvas, *Jutta and Hildegard: The Biographical Sources*, 108.

56. Ibid.

57. Despite the fact that it wasn't her official title, many people still referred to

Hildegard as abbess.

58. See Newman, ed., *Voice of the Living Light: Hildegard of Bingen and Her World*, 14.

59. James Hitchcock, *History of the Catholic Church: From the Apostolic Age to the Third Millennium* (San Francisco, CA: Ignatius Press, 2012), Kindle Edition.

60. Hildegard of Bingen, *Scivias* (The Classics of Western Spiritual Spirituality), trans. Mother Columba Hart and Jane Bishop; introduction by Barbara J. Newman; preface by Caroline Walker Bynum (New Jersey: Paulist Press, 1990), 19.

61. See Maddocks, *Hildegard of Bingen*.

62. Pope Benedict XVI, "Apostolic Letter Proclaiming Saint Hildegard of Bingen, professed nun of the Order of Saint Benedict, a Doctor of the Universal Church," October 7, 2012, accessed December 22, 2020, Vatican.va.

63. Maddocks, *Hildegard of Bingen*, quoting from Hildegard of Bingen (author) and Margaret Berger (translator), *On Natural Philosophy and Medicine: Selections from Cause et Curae* (Rochester, NY: D. S. Brewer, 1999), 100.

64. Hildegard of Bingen, *Scivias*, 12.

65. Ibid., 59–60.

66. Flanagan, *Hildegard of Bingen: A Visionary Life*, Kindle Edition.

67. Hildegard of Bingen, *Scivias*, 59.

68. Ibid.

69. Ibid., 61.

70. Carmen Acevedo Butcher, *Hildegard of Bingen: A Spiritual Reader* (Brewster, MA: Paraclete Press, 2007), Kindle Edition.

71. Meconi, *Hildegard of Bingen*, Kindle Edition.

72. Rengers and Bunson, *The 35 Doctors of the Church*.

73. Butcher, *Hildegard of Bingen: A Spiritual Reader*, Kindle Edition.

74. Régine Pernoud, *Hildegard of Bingen: Inspired Conscience of the Twelfth Century*, trans. Paul Duggan (New York: Marlowe & Co., 1998), viii.

75. Kathryn Kerby-Fulton, "Prophet and Reformer" in *Voice of the Living Light: Hildegard of Bingen and Her World*, ed. Barbara Newman, 79.

76. In her book, *Sister of Wisdom: St. Hildegard's Theology of the Feminine*, Barbara Newman explains that when Hildegard used the word "effeminate" in

a pejorative sense, she was not simply referring to the appearance of feminine traits in men, for these may be either good or bad. It is more likely that the tag denoted what is left of the feminine when its two positive attributes — virginity and maternity — have been stripped away, leaving only the generic "feminine frailty."

77. Hildegard of Bingen, *Scivias*, 12.

78. Butcher, *Hildegard of Bingen: A Spiritual Reader*, Kindle Edition.

79. See Carol Reed-Jones, *Hildegard of Bingen: Woman of Vision* (Bellingham, WA: Paper Crane Press, 2004), 12.

80. During the Second World War, these illustrations were brought to Cologne for safety and they have not been seen since. Fortunately, the nuns had made copies, which are still available today.

81. Published by Paulist Press, English translation, 539 pages.

82. The number three represents the medieval notion of perfection as reflected in the Trinity.

83. Morality plays are allegorical dramas in which the characters represent abstractions, such as the vices, virtues, death, evil, and so on, and their purpose is to teach moral lessons, to help shape Christian character in the audience.

84. Barbara Newman, *Vision: The Life and Music of Hildegard of Bingen*, ed. Jane Bobko, commentary Matthew Fox (New York: Penguin Books, 1995), 6, 9.

85. Butcher, *Hildegard of Bingen: A Spiritual Reader*, Kindle Edition.

86. Ibid.

87. The Cistercians are a monastic order founded in 1098. The order is still in existence.

88. Newman, *Vision: The Life and Music of Hildegard of Bingen*, 9.

89. Also known as Pope Eugene.

90. Meeting or assembly of bishops.

91. Pope Benedict XVI, "General Audience: Saint Hildegard of Bingen," 1 September 2010, http://w2.vatican.va/content/benedict-xvi/en/audiences/2010/documents/hf_ben-xvi_aud_20100901.html, Accessed 10 September 2019.

92. Hildegard of Bingen, *Scivias*, 13.

93. Rengers, and Bunson, *The 35 Doctors of the Church Revised Edition*, Kindle Edition.

94. Pope Benedict XVI, "General Audience: Saint Hildegard of Bingen."

95. *Jutta and Hildegard: The Biographical Sources*, trans. Silvas, 144.

96. Meconi, *Hildegard of Bingen*.

97. Ibid.

98. Newman, *Vision: The Life and Music of Hildegard of Bingen*, ed. Jane Bobko, commentary Matthew Fox, 14.

99. Baird, *The Personal Correspondence of Hildegard of Bingen*, Letter #5.

100. Reed-Jones, *Hildegard of Bingen: Woman of Vision*, 24.

101. She became Hildegard of Bingen because of the convent's proximity to the town of Bingen.

102. Written by Saint Benedict, the Rule laid down the basic organization of a monastic community and provided guidelines regarding what was needed for communal self-sufficient living, in addition to many other directives.

103. *Jutta and Hildegard: The Biographical Sources*, trans. Silvas, 101–102.

104. Marchioness von Stade's granddaughter.

105. Baird, *The Personal Correspondence of Hildegard of Bingen*, Letter #11.

106. Ibid., Letter #16.

107. More or less.

108. Baird, *The Personal Correspondence of Hildegard of Bingen*, Letter #17.

109. Ibid., Letter #18.

110. Newman, *Vision: The Life and Music of Hildegard of Bingen*, ed. Jane Bobko, commentary Matthew Fox, 14–15.

111. Julie Hotchin "The Nun's Crown," in *Early Modern Women: An Interdisciplinary Journal* 4 (2009), 187–94.

112. Tengswich's sisters, by contrast, would have their hair tied up under short black veils.

113. Butcher, *Hildegard of Bingen*.

114. Baird, *The Personal Correspondence of Hildegard of Bingen*, #5.

115. See ibid.

116. Butcher, *Hildegard of Bingen: A Spiritual Reader*.

117. Ibid.

118. Ibid.

119. Hildegard of Bingen, trans. Bruce W. Hozeski, *The Book of the Rewards of Life* (New York: Garland Publishing, Inc, 1994), back cover.

120. Ibid.

121. Butcher, *Hildegard of Bingen*.

122. Medieval books on animals, in which the real or fabulous characteristics of actually existent or imaginary animals (such as the griffin, dragon, siren, unicorn, etc.) were figuratively treated as religious symbols of Christ, the devil, the virtues, and vices. www.newadvent.org.

123. Maddocks, *Hildegard of Bingen*.

124. Meconi, *Hildegard of Bingen (Women Composers)*, Kindle Edition, quoting *Hildegard von Bingen's Physica: The Complete English Translation of Her Classic Work on Health and Healing*, trans. Pricilla Throop (Rochester, VT: Healing Arts Press, 1998), 225.

125. Régine Pernoud, trans. Paul Duggan, *Hildegard of Bingen* (New York: Marlowe & Company, 1998), 119–120.

126. Butcher, *Hildegard of Bingen*.

127. *The Book of Divine Works*, *The Book of Life's Merits*, and *Scivias*, though disparate in subject, are to be experienced as a unified trilogy.

128. Saint Hildegard of Bingen, intro. and trans. by Nathaniel M. Campbell, *Liber divinorum operum* (*The Book of Divine Works*) (Washington, D.C: The Catholic University of America Press, 2008). See International Society of Hildegard von Bingen Studies, http://www.hildegard-society.org/p/liber-divinorum-operum.html.

129. Ibid.

130. See *Jutta & Hildegard, The Biographical Sources*, trans. Silvas, 86.

131. Newman, "'Sybil of the Rhine': Hildegard's Life and Times."

132. Pope Benedict XVI, "Apostolic Letter Proclaiming Saint Hildegard of Bingen, professed nun of the Order of Saint Benedict, a Doctor of the Universal Church."

133. Rengers, and Bunson, *The 35 Doctors of the Church*.

134. Maddocks, *Hildegard of Bingen: The Woman of Her Age*, Kindle Edition. Gothic Voices is a United Kingdom-based vocal ensemble specializing in repertoire from the eleventh to the fifteenth century but also performing contemporary music, particularly pieces with medieval associations. The group's first disc, *A Feather on the Breath of God — Hymns and Sequences by Abbess Hildegard*

of Bingen, remains one of the best-selling recordings of pre-classical music ever made.

135. Owen Hopkin, "Hildegard of Bingen: life and music of the great female composer," ClassicFM.com.

136. Newman, "'Sybil of the Rhine': Hildegard's Life and Times."

137. Meconi, Hildegard of Bingen.

138. Campbell, "Re: Riesencodex," email message to Terry Polakovic, December 16, 2019.

139. See Pernoud, *Hildegard of Bingen: Inspired Conscience of the Twelfth Century*, trans. Paul Duggan, 126.

140. Sibyl is a common reference to a female oracle or prophetess.

141. Brennan Pursell, "St. Hildegard of Bingen: A Visionary for All Time" in *Crisis Magazine*, September 19, 2012.

142. *Cathars* is a Greek word meaning "pure." They were sometimes referred to as the Albigensians.

143. In reality, the Cathars were more than heretics; they were actually an opposing religion.

144. Warren H. Carroll, *The Glory of Christendom* (Front Royal, VA: Christendom Press, 1993), 165. This book is Volume 3 of the "A History of Christendom" series by Warren H. Carroll.

145. Maddocks, *Hildegard of Bingen*.

146. Hildegard of Bingen, trans. Sabina Flanagan, *Secrets of God* (Boston: Shambhala Publications, 2013). Kindle Edition, quoting *Scivias*.

147. Baird, *The Personal Correspondence of Hildegard of Bingen*. Kindle Edition, Introduction to Letter #72.

148. Barbara Newman, *Symphonia* (Ithaca, NY: Cornell University Press), 24.

149. Ibid., 25

150. Ibid.

151. Maddocks, *Hildegard of Bingen: The Woman of Her Age*, Kindle Edition.

152. *Jutta and Hildegard: The Biographical Sources*, trans. Silvas, 209. A miracle appeared in the sky over the room just as Hildegard gave up her soul to God.

153. Christopher Page, a Cambridge musicologist, is quoted by Bernard D. Sherman, https://www.bsherman.net/pageonhild.htm. See "Mistaking the Tail

for the Comet: An Interview with Christopher Page on Hildegard of Bingen." This article first appeared in *The Los Angeles Times*, Sunday, August 9, 1998. It is reprinted with permission, January 2, 2020.

154. Butcher, *Hildegard of Bingen: A Spiritual Reader*, Kindle Edition.

155. www.st-hildegard.com.

156. Brennan Pursell "St. Hildegard of Bingen: A Visionary for All Time."

157. See Reid J. Turner, "Understanding the Writings of St. Hildegard," The Five Beasts blog, accessed December 22, 2020, https://thefivebeasts.wordpress.com /understanding-the-writings-of-st-hildegard/.

158. Rengers, and Bunson, *The 35 Doctors of the Church*.

159. See Pope Francis, *On Hope*, Kindle Edition.

CONCLUSION

1. By the French philosopher, Paul Ricoeur. https://holyhillocdscommunity. weebly.com/uploads/1/4/2/1/14214286/keith_egan_teresa_of_avila_hope__2. pdf

2. Haley Stewart, "The Hope of the Domestic Church," *Evangelization Culture: The Journal of the Word on Fire Institute*. Issue No 6/hope. Winter 2020, 81.

3. Peter Seewald, "Benedict & Hope," *Evangelization Culture: The Journal of the Word on Fire Institute*. Issue No 6/hope. Winter 2020, 96.

4. Haley Stewart, "The Hope of the Domestic Church," 80.

5. Peter Seewald, "Benedict & Hope," 96.

6. Ibid.

7. *Evangelization Culture: The Journal of the Word on Fire Institute*, 69.

About the Author

Terry Polakovic lives in Denver, Colorado, with her husband, Mike. She is the cofounder of Endow (Educating on the Nature and Dignity of Women) and served as the president of the organization from 2003 to 2015. Before retiring, she worked in nonprofit leadership for more than thirty years. In 2010, she received the Pro Ecclesia et Pontiface Cross Award ("For the Church and the Pontiff") from Pope Benedict XVI. In 2011, Terry was recognized as an "Outstanding Catholic Leader" by the Catholic Leadership Institute. She is the author of *Life and Love: Opening Your Heart to God's Design*, published by Our Sunday Visitor in 2018.